DEVELOPMENT OF EDUCATION IN INDIA

Published by
Saurabh Publishing House

DEVELOPMENT OF EDUCATION IN INDIA

Anita Vats

Saurabh
Publishing House
4263 / 3, Ansari Road,
Daryaganj, New Delhi-110002

Published by :
SAURABH PUBLISHING HOUSE

Distributed by :
LOTUS PRESS
4263/3, Ansari Road, Darya Ganj, New Delhi-110002
Ph : 32903912, 23280047
E-Mail : lotus_press@sify.com

Saurabh Publishing is an imprint of
Lotus Press

ISBN : 978-81-89005-21-4 (H.B.)

Printed in India by Anand Sons, Delhi

PREFACE

Education in India had its beginnings in the need to satisfy man's innate curiosity, while he lived in the lap of nature. It is usually argued that the elements, methodology and organisation of education in India originated during the Vedic period, but the truth is that the highly developed form the Pre-Vedic civilization, *i.e.*, the civilization of Mohen-jo-Daro, or the civilization of the Indus valley, points to the fact that man could not have achieved this degree of development without the growth of education. The Aryan period is regarded as the healthy, peaceful, mature and practical age of education. As Dr. Altekar has put it, "From the Vedic age downwards the central concept of education of the Indians has been that it is a source of illumination, giving us a correct lead in the various spheres of life."

India's educational and cultural traditions are the most ancient in the world's history. All that India is today, is the gift of its cultural and social heritage of the last 5000 years. In ancient India, the traditions of society and the nation were preserved in schools. At that time, means of public communication did not exist, but contacts and relations were strengthened through schools.

This book deals with the topics of—Development of Education in Vedic Period; Education During Muslims; Religion and Education; Primary Education; Basic Education System; Education in Public Schools; Higher Education; Aims of Educations; Women Education; Vocational Education in

India; Computer and Internet Education; Teacher Education; Adult Education; Promotion of Education; National Education Policy etc.

I hope that students and those in the educational field will find it useful for academic and competitive examinations. I owe a deep sense of gratitude to my publisher for materialising my present endeavour.

ANITA VATS

Contents

1

Development of Education in Vedic Period

To attain salvation by realising the truth has been the aim of education, during this period. Only that education was regarded true which helped one to realise this supreme truth. According to the *Upanishads* 'truth' alone is the knowledge and the other worldly knowledge is untruth. The worldly knowledge was regarded as ignorance. *Upanishads* maintain that one cannot attain salvation through worldly knowledge because through this one becomes involved in illusion (Maya).

Upanayan Sanskar. Upanayan Sanskar was considered important both in the Vedic and Post-Vedic periods. This is evident at several places in the Rigveda. But different values were adhered to in the two periods. It was not necessary during the Vedic period to have the Upanayan ceremony before starting education. But during the Post-Vedic period Upanayan ceremony was considered necessary for starting education.

The word 'Upanayan' means to come near. In the context of education this word signifies that the student should come near the teacher for receiving education. The Upanayan ceremony became so important during the Post-Vedic period that it was usually regarded as second birth of the individual. For the Brahmans this became very important. Brahmans began to be called as Dvij (the twice born or born again). It was after the Upanayan that a Brahman boy could be called a Dvij.

Two births signify the worldly and the spiritual births. On the Upanayan occasion the Guru (preceptor) used to give him his Mantra (Advice). His spiritual life used to begin from this point. That is, from this day his education was started which ultimately led to his spiritual development in due course of time. The Upanayan ceremony is still in vogue in certain religious groups in the world, though in different forms.

The Important Place of the Teacher. During this period the teacher (Guru) enjoyed a predominant place not only in his Gurukul (seat of learning) but in the entire society. He was regarded as a great guide for all. To his pupils he showered all love and affection and used to teach them whatever he knew, but before doing this he always tested the deservingness of a particular pupil. The pupils were free to discuss any points freely with the Guru. We find many examples of free discussion between the teacher and his disciple. We may cite here an example from Brahma and his son Bhrigu. Brahma gave the Brahma-gyan, *i.e.*, the knowledge of the ultimate or God in an outline form and advised him to perceive the same through thinking (Manan) and meditation. Bhrigu accepted this advice and realised God (Brahma) on the basis of the same.

Curriculum During the Post-Vedic Period. During this period the curriculum included more subjects than during the Vedic age. Veda mantras (Vedic hymns and verses) were principally taught in the Vedic period. During the Post-Vedic period various types of literatures were produced pertaining to the different Vedas. In addition to religious subjects many worldly subjects were also included in the curriculum. This may be verified in the conversation between Narrad and Sanat Kumar which is incorporated in the Chhandogya

Upanishad. During the Post-Vedic period the curriculum consisted of Vedas, History, Puranas, Grammar, Mathematics, Brahma-Vidya, Nirukti (etymological interpretation of words), Astronomy, Dance, Music, etc.

In addition to the above three methods we find a mention of another method—question-answer system in the Upanishad literature. In fact, the entire Upanishad literature is on the question-answer system. We do not find its practice in the Rigvedic period. Through this system difficult and abstract ideas were made simple. The terse-spiritual elements were explained through this system. Examples, strories and help of certain biographies were also taken in the system for elucidating certain points. This question-answer method was also successfully used by Socrates in Greece to explain abstract ideas.

Daily Routine of Students. During the Post-Vedic period the Ashramas (schools) were generally organised and run by Gurus (preceptors). It was compulsory to adhere to laid down rules of discipline and conduct. No distinction was made between students in this respect. Everyone was required to observe celibacy. Rules of conduct were enforced keeping in view the physical, mental and moral development of students. Strict adherence to rules of conduct and discipline was an inseparable aspect of education in those days.

(a) ***Practical Education.*** Practical education consisted of three parts : *1.* to beg alms, *2.* to prepare fire for the Yajna-kund, and *3.* to look after the animals and other fellow-beings of the Ashrama (School). Besides, the students were also expected to do some agricultural work.

There were varying aims of all these three aspects of practical education. Begging of alms was meant to teach politeness. Preparing of fire for the Yajna-kund signified mental development of students.

Rearing up Ashrama animals and doing agricultural work were meant to make the students self-dependent.

(b) ***Moral Education.*** Leading a disciplined and controlled life is the real basis of moral education. Moral education affects the conduct of the individual. Only oral instruction cannot improve one's conduct. Therefore, observance of celibacy was considered necessary for good conduct.

(c) ***Mental Development.*** Hearing, thinking and meditation were the three parts of mental education. For full mental development all these three aspects were considered necessary. Thinking over the heard things and perception through meditation were the accepted methods of mental development. This is true even today.

Teacher's Place in the Ancient Indian Society. In the ancient Indian society the teacher always enjoyed a dignified place. During the Vedic and Post-Vedic periods the teacher's place was second to that of God only. He was more respected than the king in society. The Guru-Ashrama was known as the Gurukul (the family of the teacher) and the Guru was regarded as a rishi (sage) or Acharya (the one who practises what he professes). The Guru was given this significant place, because without him it was impossible to attain knowledge. The Guru was the guide and could help anyone to carve out his course of action. He used to bring light wherever there was darkness. Thus the people always felt his necessity whenever there was a difficulty in solving any issue or problem.

During the Upanishadic period as well, when self-study was considered as dignified the place of Guru in society remained intact. It was believed that no knowledge could come without the assistance from the Guru. In other words, it was believed that the attainment of salvation was not possible without the help of the Guru.

Restriction on Teachers. The teacher was expected to lead a life of penance free of worldly things. He, too, was required to follow all the rules of strict discipline, thinking and meditation which were prescribed for the students. We find many references to such a position in the Maitrayan Upanishad. After the demise of the Guru even one of his disciples could succeed him if his son was not considered worthy of the same.

Women's Education. Many changes were introduced in women's education during the Post-Vedic period. This led to the fall of women's education. During the Vedic age the women enjoyed equal educational rights. During the Post-Vedic period they were deprived of the social and religious rights. They were not allowed to participate in social functions. Now they did not enjoy the same status as before. Thus the path of their social and mental development was blocked. Ultimately the position of women in society fell down so low that the birth of a girl was regarded as a curse on the family.

But an upward trend again appeared in the status of women during the Upanishadic period. Now they were given social and educational rights again. Once again they were given equal status with men and many women bacame as learned as men. Many women became Acharya (Principal teacher-Guru) in Ashramas. The name of Gargi may be cited as an example.

Convocation Address. After receiving education for twelve years students used to assemble near their teacher (Acharya) for blessings before going home. The Acharya on this occasion used to give some pieces of advice for happy and smooth running of their future life. The teacher used to tell them how to lead a life of householder (Grihastha), how to take care of the society and the nation and how to serve the humanity as a whole. The teacher used to tell all these in a ceremony which was known as Samavartan Samaroha like the modern convocation address.

Varna System and Education in Society. The Varna system in the Vedic age was based on one's work or duty (Karma). Members of a family used to engage themselves in different types of work (profession) and their work decided their varna. During the Vedic period one could choose a particular profession as he liked and accordingly his Varna was determined. But during the Post-Vedic period Varna came to be determined by birth. Consequently, the whole society was divided into four Varnas—Brahman, Kshatriya, Vaishya and Shudra.

Out of these four Varnas, the Brahmans occupied the supreme position and enjoyed more rights. Kshatriyas resented this superiority and a clash ensued between the two. Kshatriya were the winners in the clash and the administrative powers came into their hands. Gradually they established their kingdoms and principalities. Thus in the Varna system the Brahmans and the Kshatriyas became predominant. The Vaishyas and Shudras came into the lower groups. In this hierarchy Shudras were kept at the lowest order of society. In course of time the condition of Shudras fell down further and they came to be regarded as untouchables and they were denied all social and religious rights. Vaishyas remained superior to Shudras and they divided themselves into professional groups such as—goldsmith, blacksmith, potter, fowler, milkman and sweet-seller etc., etc.

However, the position of Varnas during the Post-Vedic period had not degenerated so much as it is found today. At that time, it was possible to change one's Varna. One could marry a girl from a different Varna. The Vaishyas were permitted in the Rajya Surya Yajna upto some extent. Then, Brahmans also did not control the Yajnas. The marriages of

Chyavan Rishi and King Shantanu and the religious rites performed by Vishwamitra (A Kshatriya) and other Kshatriyas bear a testimony to the above.

The Post-Vedic literature does not contain much about the education of Vaishyas and Shudras. Agriculture was the main occupation of Vaishyas during this period.

Characteristics of Education

Such terms as knowledge, awakening, humility, modesty, etc. are often used to characterise education in the Vedic period. Ancient texts refer to the uneducated person as an ignorant beast. Education is regarded as the source of light. The main features of Vedic education can be briefly enumerated as follows:

1. Knowledge. Education is knowledge. It is man's third eye. This aphorism means that knowledge opens man's inner eye, flooding him with spiritual and divine light, which forms the provision for man's journey through life. Through education, the development of every aspect of human life becomes possible. Knowledge protects an individual like a mother, inspires him to follow the path of good conduct as a father does, and gives the pleasure that one's wife provides.

Education leads to the development of personality. The word 'Veda' originates from the root 'vid' which bears the meaning of knowledge. Sayana declares that the Veda is a means to the obtaining of the adorced that which is worthy of worship, as well as a means to the banishment of the underised, the evil. Knowledge of the four Vedas (Rigveda, Yajurveda, Samaveda, and Atharvaveda), along with the knowledge of Shruti, Smriti, etc., provided an individual, with new knowledge which broadened his inteclletual horizon.

2. Alms of Education. In the Vedic period, education had an idealistic form, in which the teachers (acharyas) laid stress upon worship of God, religiousness, spirituality, formation of character, development of personality, creation of an aptitude for the development of culture, nation and society. It is in this context that Dr. Altekar said that the objectives of education in ancient India were worship of God, a feeling for religion, formation of character, fulfilment of public and civic duties, an increase in social efficiency or skill, and the protection the propagation of national culture. These objectives and ideals took an individual along the path of spiritual development. In their fundamental form, these objectives and ideals were:

(i) ***Emphasis upon Knowledge and Experience.*** The Gurukuls laid emphasis upon knowledge and obtaining of experience. During the Vedic period, the practice of distributing degrees did not exist. Students exhibited the knowledge obtained through discourses and discussions conducted in a concourse of scholars.

(ii) ***Spirituality.*** In the Vedic period, nature was regarded as divine and worshipped. During this period, many hypotheses concerning spirituality took birth. Knowledge came to be seen as the instrument of salvation. Fire sacrifices, fasting and taking of vows became a part of life. Education was given the objective of inculcating control over these aspects and learning right conduct based on them.

(iii) ***Fulfilment of Duty.*** Great importance was attached to developing such qualities as discipline, obedience, performance of hostly duties, rendering help to others, fulfilment of social responsibilities, etc. Through such education social skills were developed in the students. In addition, education was also provided for earning a livelihood, and for this, one or more skills were taught. Dr. Mukerjee says that this education was not exclusively theortical or literary. It was related to one or the other manual skill.

(iv) ***Sublimation of Instincts.*** Man is the virtual slave of the instinctive drives embedded in his psyche, and when he is obsessed by his senses, he often adopts the wrong path. The objective of education was to sublimate these instinctive tendencies, to turn the mind away from material knowledge, and centre it upon the spiritual world, thus establishing control over materialistic and base tendencies.

(v) ***Growth of Character and Personality.*** The objective of education was the formation of character and personality of children. It was achieved through an appropriate environment, lessons on right conduct, and teachings based on the life, character and ideals of great persons. Education aimed at developing the virtues of self-control, self-respect, love, cooperation, sympathy, etc. in the students.

3. The 'Upnayana' Ritual. The word 'Upnayana' means to take close to, or to bring in touch with. A ceremony called the Upnayana ceremony was performed before the child was taken to his teacher. This ceremony was performed at the ages of 8, 11 and 12 for the brahmins, kshatriyas and vaishyas, respectively. The ceremony signalled the childs's transition from infancy to childhood, and his initiation into educational life. In this context, the term 'Upnayana' means putting the student in touch with his teacher. With the passage of time, the ceremony came to be confined to the brahmin class only.

4. The Method of Education. During the Vedic period, the Gurukul method prevailed, in which the student lived in the house of the Guru, instead of living with his parents. Along with his colleagues, he led a celibate life and obtained education in the house of the Guru. Initially, in the Vedic period, it was the teacher who occupied the primary place, but in the later period, it was the student who occupied the central place in education, the process of education passed through the three stages of comprehension, meditation, memory and nidhi-dhyaasana. The Gurukuls were the centres of education, in which education was imparted only by individuals of character and ability. The student remained with his Guru for 12 years. There were parishads or committees to satisfy the student's thirst for knowledge.

5. Celibacy or Brahmacharya. Every student was required to observe celibacy in his specific path of life. Purity of conduct was regarded as of supreme importance. Only the unmarried could become students in a Gurukul. On entering student life, the student was made to wear a special girdle called a 'makhla'. Its quality depended on the caste of the student. Brahmins wore a girdle of moonj grass, the kshatriyas of string gut-taanta—and the vaishyas a girdle made of wool. The clothes worn by them were also accordingly of silk, wool, etc. The students were not allowed to make use of fragrant, cosometic or intoxicating things.

6. Service of the Teacher. Every student was required, while residing in the Gurukul, to serve his teacher compulsorily. Any violation of the Guru's instructions was regarded as a sin, and subject to stern punishment. The student's duties included obtaining such daily necessities as water, a twig for brushing the teeth, etc., for his guru. The teachers also ensured that the students should not be distracted from their studies while performing such duties.

7. Alms System. The student had to bear the responsibility of feeding both himself and his teacher, this was done through begging for alms, which was not considered bad, since every domestic knew that his own son must be begging for alms in the same way at some other place. The reason behind the introduction of such a practice was that accepting alms induces humility. The student realised that both education and subsequent earning of livelihood were made possible for him only through society's service and its sympathy. For the poor students, begging for alms was compulsory and unavoidable, but even among the prosperous, it was a generally accepted practice.

The work of teaching began early in the morning. After performing their ablutions, students participated in some religious rituals, such as havans. Subsequently, they were put to the task of studying. In the afternoon, after partaking of lunch, the students returned to their studies. At sunset, some more religious rituals were performed. They denoted the end of the day's routine.

8. Practicality. The education of that period encompassed the necessary activities of life. Students were given education about animal-husbandry, agriculture and other professions. In addition education in medicine was also imparted. According to Dr. Alteker, the purpose of education was not to provide general knowledge about a variety of subjects, but to produce specialists of the best kind in various spheres.

9. Duration of Education. In the house of the teacher, the student was required to obtain education upto the age of 24, after which he was expected to enter domestic life. Students were divided into three categories:

(a) Those obtaining education upto the age of 24—Vasu.

(b) Those obtaining education upto the age of 36—Rudra.

(c) Those obtaining education upto the age of 48—Aaditya.

10. Education for the Individual. In the Vedic period, every teacher devoted himself to the integral development of each student. He aimed at the physical and intellectual development of his wards. The maximum attention was devoted to the individual development of every student, but there was no provision for the education of the incapable and the handicapped, especially those who were lacking in mental and moral qualities or were known for moral turpitude.

11. Curriculum. Although the education of this period was dominated by the study of Vedic literature, historical study, stories of heroic lives and discourses on the Puranas also formed a part of the syllabus. Students had necessarily to obtain knowledge of metrics. Arithmetic was supplemented by a knowledge of geometry. Students were given knowledge of the four Vedas—Rigveda, Yajurveda, Samaveda and Atharvaveda. The syllabus took with in its compass such subjects as spiritual as well as materialistic knowledge, Vedas, Vedic grammar, arithmetic, knowledge of gods, knowledge of the absolute, knowledge of ghosts, astronomy, logic, philosophy, ethics, conduct, etc. The richness of the syllabus was responsible for the creation of Brahman literature in this period.

❐

2

Education During Muslims

With the emergence of Islam, the attention of Muslim kings turned towards India. Time was kind to them. It allowed them to settle themselves firmly in this country. After the Gulam, Khilji, Tuglak, Sayyed and Lodhi dynasties, Mogul kings established many educational institutions in India. This education, too, had its roots in religion. During this period, Indian art and culture came under the influence of Arab culture and civilization. It was only natural that the same political influence should also have made itself felt. In consequence, education too came under this influence. Islam had its origin between 570 A.D. and 632 A.D. Hazrat Mohammed collected his messages in the Holy Quran, and this text came to be an instrument of social direction for the Muslim kings. During this period, these kings made arrangements for education in order to serve their own interests. Mohammed Gauri started his aggressions on India, but at the same time, he also had mosques and schools constructed in Ajmer to make arrangements for education in Islam and Muslim law. His successor Kutubuddin also followed in his footsteps. The other rulers of his dynasty, Altamesh, Razia Begum, Nasiruddin, Balban and others also had mosques, maktabs and schools established with government aid.

Ferozshah Tuglak of the Tuglak dynasty made efforts for the propagation of education. One of the schools established by him in Delhi has been described as follows. The school was located in a large ground and a big building with massive towers. It was situated in a garden in which human skill harmonized with nature, thus creating an environment most suitable for contemplation and thought. Near the school was a lake, whose water shone like silver. The grand building of the school was reflected in its waters. It was an enchanting sight to see hundreds of students crossing the polished and soomth floors and congregating round their teachers.

During the reign of Sikander Lodi (1489-1519), Indians, too, had begun to learn Persian (Pharsi). After obtaining knowledge of this laguage, they began to work in government departments. The Muslim rulers themselves felt the need for Hindu workers in the administrative sphere, and hence they made arrangements for the study of Indian languages. And, as a result of the contact between the Hindus and Muslims, Urdu, which was the spoken form of Persian mixed with Hindi, was evolved. The Mughal rulers who followed the earlier Muslim rulers had relatively greater interest in education, and hence it was in this later period that education developed more adequately. Akbar authorised the translation of many important Indian texts, including the Mahabharata, the Ramayana, Atharvaveda and Lilawati, into Persian. Akbar's deep interest in education is high-lighted by Abul Fazal's comments in his famous work '*Aaiyene Akbari*' to the effect that in every country, and especially in India, boys were kept in school for years where they were taught about consonants and vowels. Since they had to read numberous books, a large part of the boys' time was wasted. Emperor Akbar declared that each student should be taught to write the alphabet in various ways. Each student was required to learn the name of every letter (varna) within two days. Emphasis was laid upon imparting education in moral values, arithmetic, political arithmetic, agriculture, medicine, logic, and physical, mathematical and divine philosophy to every student.

Jehangir went so far as to enact a law that the property and wealth of any person dying without an heir would be utilized for the repair of schools and religious buildings. Shahjahan had a university established near the Jama Masjid. Auraugzeb did propagate Muslim education, but at the same time he destroyed Hindu schools and temples. He granted excessive facilities for Muslim students, but he accorded a low status to teachers. After the collapse of the Mughal Empire, schools suffered a severe blow. Many such institutions closed down due to anarchy and lack of finances. According to Vakil and Natrajan—"It must be noted that while mosques, maktabs and madrassas sprang up with the spread of Mohammadan power and provided facilities for Islamic learning in different parts of the country, the Hindu system of education continued to prevail in pathashalas, maths and temples except where their work was disturbed or dislocated by Mohammadan inroads or invasions." One finds a lack of organisation in Muslim education. In the Muslim period, education was founded on community basis. Hence, it is illogical to claim that the Muslim ruler sought to propagate education liberally.

Bernier, the famous French traveller who visited India during this period, observed that during the period which he had described, it was only natural to find deep and universal ignorance. Was it possible to establish suitably financially aided schools and colleges or other centres of education in India? Where would the organisers be found? And, even if they were found, from where would the students be obtained? He also observed the absence of individuals whose wealth was adequate for providing suitable aid to colleges. And, even if such individuals existed, he felt that no one had the courage to compel them to bring out their wealth for such an investment. He felt that even some individual did venture on such a foolish act, there was an absence of religious places, enterprises and offices with employment potential which could utilize the ability and science imparted to students, and thus serve as an inspiration for youth to be hopeful and to compete for future success.

Characteristics of Muslim Education

During the Muslim period, education developed so slowly that no notable characteristic of it ever emerged. Minor rulers had educational institutions established for the satisfaction of their interests. However, the following features can be noted:

1. Encouragement by the State. Muslim rulers took an interest in education, and so they provided aid to maktabs and madrassas. There were granted jagirs or landed property. Scholars were given places of eminence in the courts of kings. The rulers started giving aid to madrassas and maktabs being run in or along with mospues. Hence, their propagation of education was communal.

2. Arabic and Persian. During this period, special stress was laid on the teaching of Arabic and Persian, which were made the media of education by Muslim rulers. Knowledge of these two languages was essential for securing employment in government offices. Consequently, Hindus too began to learn Arabic and Persian.

3. Materialism. Muslim education sought the spread of education only from the practical and materialistic viewpoints. Education in manual skills, sculpture, agriculture, medicine, etc., is proof of this. In addition to religious education, teachers tried to ensure that after receiving education, the child should become capable of earning his livelihood. Consequently, knowledge of military science, painting, sculpture, housing construction, manufacture of weapons, etc., was also imparted. Knowledge of such subjects was given to students directly and individually by experts through a system of apprenticeship.

4. Emergence of Urdu. The evolution of the new language 'Urdu' which emerged from the inter-mixing of Arabic and Persian, is the greatest contribution of the Mughal period. The importance that this language enjoys today is due entirely to the Muslim period.

5. Religious Influence. The education of this period was profoundly influenced by Islam. Every Muslim sought education for the purpose of searching for knowledge and for religious purposes. There is direct evidence of the influence of Islam on the education of this period. Students were required to memorise the Koran. Importance was attached to study of Islam. This religious influence upon education was positive proof of the communal attitude of Muslim rulers.

6. Development of History-Writing. By initiating the writing of the history of their period, Muslim rulers helped to develop the art of writing history. Both Mughal and Muslim rulers commissioned the writing of the histories of their period or reigns. Among the most famous of these are Babar Nama, Akbar Nama, etc.

Centres of Education

The political organisation of the Muslim rulers was decentralised. The Mansabdars, kings, zamindars or landlords, etc., became dependent rulers of their individual areas after paying the requisite tax to royal treasury. These rulers had mosques constructed, and soon the mosques changed into maktabs and madrassas. During the Muslim period, Agra, Delhi, Jaunpur, Lahore, Ajmer, Bidar, Lucknow, Ferozabad, Jullundur, Multan, Bijapur, etc., became important centres of education.

1. Agra. Agra was founded by Sikandar Lodi. He had the town established as a centre of Islamic education, and it soon took the form of a university. Hundreds of madrassas in this town provided education in literature, mathematics, philosophy, medicine, etc. Later on, Akbar, Jehangir and Shahjahan also contributed to the development of education in this town.

2. Bidar. Bidar, too, was an important educational centre. Mahmood Gawan had a huge madrassas and a library established here. Later, Alauddin Ahmed contributed to the development of education.

3. Delhi. Delhi was renowned far and wide as a centre of Muslim education. Nasiruddin established the Nasaria Madrassas here. The Gulam dynasty also helped the spread of education in Delhi. During the reign of Alauddin Khilji, 34 famous scholars of Islam lived in Delhi. Feroz Tuglak had 30 madrassas established. Humayun opened madrassas for imparting knowledge of astrology and geography. Akbar, Jehangir, Shahjahan and Aurangazeb also established various madrassas for imparting knowledge of various specific fields.

4. Jaunpur. During the reign of Feroz, Jaunpur was a prominent centre of Muslim education. It had many schools imparting education in the arts, literature and other spheres of knowledge. The Sharkias made valuable contributions to the development of education. Sher Shah Suri himself was a student here.

In addition to the above centres, there were at least one maktab and one madarsa in every village of Bijapur, Golkunda, Malwa, Khandesh, Multan, Gujrat, Lucknow, Sialkot and Bengal.

System of Education

During the Muslim period, the system of education was organised in the following manner:

1. Bismillah. Education began with the performance of the ritual known as 'Bismillah', which was performed at the age of 4 years, 4 months and 4 days. It was similar to the

Upnayan ceremony of the Vedic period and the Pabbaja ritual of the Buddhist period. On this day, the child was adorned with a new crown and sent to his teacher, the Maulvi, where the latter inaugurated the child's education with a recitation from the Koran. Affluent people had this ritual performed at home.

2. Maktab. Education began in the maktab, i.e., a primary school. The teachers called Maulvis taught the alphabet along with verses from the Koran. The child's primary education took place in these schools. Generally, most such maktabs were appendages of mosques. The child was taught writing, the Koran, namaz or prayer, azaan, arithmetic, drafting, conversation, letter-writing, etc.

3. Madrassa. Madrassas provided higher education to the students. They were aided by the government. Here higher education was imparted through lectures. There were arrangements for hostels in the madrassas. They were owned privately as well as by the state.

4. Method of Teaching. Emphasis was placed on memorisation in addition to reading, writing and arithmetic. The most prevalent method was the oral. Individual attention was paid to students. The monitor system had been used in maktabs and madrassas.

5. Syllabus. The syllabus of education in the Muslim period included such subjects as the holy Koran, the biography of Hazrat Mohammed Sahib, the history and the laws of Islam, Arabic and Persian, grammar, literature, logic, philosophy, law, astrology, history, geography, agriculture, Unani system of medicine, etc. There were provisions for teaching Sanskrit to Hindu children. Madrassas provided both religious and material or worldly education. Subjects of religious education included Koran, Islamic laws, history and Sufi philosophy, while worldly or material education consisted of grammar, language, literature, etc. There were some specialized centres for education in particular subjects.

6. Student-Teacher Relationship. During this period, relations between students and teachers were not marked by intimacy, but there were no doubts about sincerity and purity. Though teachers received a low salary, they had an important place in society. People respected them and bestowed faith on them. The teacher had a paternal attitude towards his wards. It was believed that the students who served their teachers made God happy. Despite this, there was nothing notable in this relationship. Aurangzeb is known to have insulted his teacher Mulla Shah Saleh.

7. Medium of Education. During the Muslim period, Arabic and Persian were the media of education. However, after the growth of Urdu, education began to be imparted through this language.

8. Reward and Punishment. There was a system of severe punishment to maintain order and discipline, but brilliant scholars were also rewarded.

Merits of Muslim Education

1. Compulsory. Education was compulsory, specially for boys.

2. Co-ordination. There was proper co-ordination between religious values and material or worldly needs and well-being.

3. Character. Great stress was laid on character building.

4. Incentives. There was arrangement for rewards and scholarships for meritorious and intelligent students. This provided an incentive to learning and education.

5. Literature. Under Muslim rulers, through educational system, a good deal of development of literature took place.

6. Free. The education during the Muslim rule was mostly free.

7. Practical. Great stress was laid on practical utility.

8. Personal Touch. There was a personal touch between the teacher and the taught.

9. Institutions. During this period, great attention was paid towards establishment of educational institutions. Prospersous people were encouraged to establish institutions.

10. Curriculum. Curriculum included arrangement for the teaching of various subjects.

11. Special Centres. There were centres of specialized education.

12. Writing of History. During this period, the tendency to write history was developed. This tendency was different from the tendency of the ancient India. It helped preservation of record.

Demerits of Muslim Education

1. Unsuitable. Unsuitability was characteristic of the institution of education.

2. Material. There was predominance of material considerations.

3. Disbalance. Education of the Hindus was neglected. This brought about a disbalanced development of education.

4. One-sided Curricula. There was too much emphasis on teaching Arabic and Persian. This led to neglect of other subjects.

5. Wrong Methods of Teachings. Oral or verbal method of teaching did not help the consolidation of the knowledge.

6. Lack of Co-ordination. There was no co-ordination between reading and writing.

7. Low Status of Teachers. The teacher-taught relationship was not ideal. The teacher did not occupy that position that he occupied during the Vedic period.

8. No Development of Reasoning. No encouragement to students to develop their power of reasoning.

9. Defective Curriculum. Curriculum was defective.

10. Indifference Towards Women Education.

11. Lack of Psychological Basis. Muslim education lacked psychological incentives.

12. No Universal Education. There was no provision for universal education.

❐

3

Religion and Education

The most developed period from the view point of religion has been the Vedic period when religion was considered as a basis for human life and source of inspiration for virtuous conduct. Since then religion has been inspiring people to follow the right path, improve their conduct and imbibe human virtues. It is possible that certain superstitutions, conservation, frustrations, fears and doubts might have crept into religion due to some ignorance. Self-confidence has always been with man in the form of religion. Religion by adding to the human qualities, has made man capable of self-confidence, self-reform, self-realisation, self-discipline, self-reliance and self-development.

Vedas are the oldest books. Vedas are the repository of all knowledge. Here in religion has been described in its wider perspective. According to the Vedas, the efforts, which inspire man for various conduct and develop human qualities, fall in the category of religion. Hence, than in characteristic of religion is inspiration for virtuous conduct. The modern word 'Religion' can not be a synonym for 'Dharm', bacause 'Dharm' has been considered as all-pervading in Indian scriptures. All activities from rising in the morning to sleeping a night and death and actions after death are all included in 'Dharm'. In fact, whatever qualities a person acquires are his Dharm. Here qualities mean human qualities which are universal.

In Islam 'mazhab' is a way of imparting education for virtuous conduct. According to the philosophy of this religion, 'namaz', 'Roja' and 'Haj' are considered, a method for creating universal love and feeling of neighbourhood. To give some benefit to the society or social service are considered as a part of this religion.

Some narrow minded people evince unnecessary opposition by equaling religion with sects. We should clearly understand the meaning of religion and sects. Religion is taken in the wider sense which means spiritual development of human society through the welfare of mankind. In other words; religion means human religion which every society is prepared to accept. A sect (belief) is a specific religious view point of a group of persons. That is the individual belief of the persons of that group, based on the wider values of religion. It is not necessary for other sects to accept that belief. Hindu religion accepts the opinion of Vedas, Islam that of the Quran and Christians of Bible. Hindu Dharm has been divided into Buddha sect, Jains, Sikh, Vedic (Sanatan and Arya Samaj) according to the different methods to philosophers and thinkers of these sects, although all these sects are parts of Hindu Dharm. Some agitators and diplomats propagated it as different religions in order to create faction in Hindu Dharm. The idea behind this propaganda was to cut of the organisation and unity of Hindu Dharm. It is amazing that some Hindus also accepted the sects as different religions.

Islam Dharm has its original form the word 'Salm'. 'Salm' means peace which has been interpreted as knowing God peacefully and surrendering the self before Him. This is the true nature of Islam. Whenever some one seeks the shelter of God, forgetting his vanity and pride, he attain all-round development and divinity is rediated from his personality. In Christian religion, christianity was formed from the word 'christos' which means 'bathed in Divine wisdom'. Thus christian religion extends that divine wisdom which creates brotherhood, love, sympathy and tolerance in the human society.

Vedic religion, is based on Vedas, 'Ved' means knowledge. Hence Vedic Dharm means that scientific knowledge which by recognising the existence of 'Inner self' and 'Supreme self' *i.e.* 'Antaratma' and 'Parmatma', develops human qualities like, non-violence, truth, humanism, love and compassion, etc. Thus religion is a source of morality. Science can be of great help in this direction, but science devoid of religion is meaningless. Religion is all-pervading and Universal. So it should be included in education.

Due to ignorance and superstitutions some universe followers of religions have strangulated humanity and have committed great atrocities. The reason for such violent attitude is misinterpretation of religion. These religions hypocrises of violent nature committed so many atrocities on humanity that man began to hate religion. These committing oppressions in the name of religion were non-vedic (unwise) and selfish. Religious reformers born from time to time led the people to the right path and presented the true nature of religion like, Buddha, Mahavir, Shankaracharya, Dayanand, etc., were such great personalities. In the Western countries Rousseau and Locke suggested to save education from wrongly interpreted religion. Corrupt practice, in various religious bodies in the name of religion created hatred for religion.

Relation Between Religion and Education

Religion and Education are closely associated with each other both are of spiritual tendencies. Spiritual, material or physical urge are dealt with by religion as well as by the education. "Both seek to emancipate man, not from contract with his environment, but from slavery to it." As has already been discussed, *education creates certain values of life and help in the modification of behaviour*. It gives certain mouldings to the life, while religion beautifies the life by cultivation of truthful heart with the moral and spiritual values.

In this way religion and education have different ways but the same aim of achieving God through cultivating three absolutes truth, religion and goodness. Religion must be given a suitable places in the curriculum because it is the core of our culture and 'heritage'. Gentle given a fine statement in regard to the place of religion in the curriculum.

Gentle says : "National cultures have never been more conscious than now of the higher needs of the mind, needs that are not only aesthetic and abstractly intellectual but also ethical and religious. For a school without an ethical and religious constant is an absurdity." Thus, religion should find a suitable and proper place in the sphere of education. Education, according to Pestalozzi, is aimed at "natural harmonious and progressive development of man's innate powers." Wider education mean an education which broadens the outlook, awakens the inner powers and teaches us to respect all the religions. In this manner, a teacher should enable the pupils to cultivate religious attitude and mentality through education. Religion, in this sense does not mean merely a bundle of rites and of dogmas followed by symbols and emotions but it is applied to all that what noble. Religion and education with this collective and mutual efforts lead a person towards self-realization and self-understanding. Rousseau and Wordsworth believed in nature and education on the lane; of nature. The essence of their philosophy was to worship nature in practical way.

Truly speaking, religious education does not mean something separable but pure, honest and beneficial. Education is nothing but religion, because both the religion and the education aim at harmonising the person to the ultimate truth. Religion is the pure form of education.

Education has been defined as "a process of development in which consists the passage of human being from infancy, to Maturity, the process by which he adopts himself gradually in various ways to his physical and spiritual environment." In this definition the ability of social adaptation means the development of the social qualities like co-operation, co-ordination among social groups and communities. This ability of the adaptation is religious, because religion in a wider sense says clearly that all are one. We are brothers and sisters borne of the same father. The same ideology of co-operation is found in this interpretation alike education.

What is man and what is God? These are the main problems dealt with by religion. These are the truth of a vital significance and are at the basis "of the whole structure of knowledge whether of fact or value, and deprived of them education as well as life is radically defective, without centre, balance or proper subordination of part to part."

The aim of education is all-round development of man. The same is the aim of religion. So because use of this common aim the corelation of education and religion quite natural. Now to include the various forms of religion in education, is a great problem. Some people due to their ignorance of the true nature of religion, do not and to give any place to religion in education, whereas some people want to give it an important place. Since earliest times in India, education and religion have been related to each other. With the break of this relation, indiscipline, violence and immorality have increased. According to Dr. Sarvapalli Radhakrishnan the reason for all vices and troubles pervading the world is want of morality which has been created due to education being not corelated to religion. Here in India there were those centres of education in which people from all parts of the world came to receive education. In Western countries also Movements were started for, educational organisation by correlating religion and education. Sunday School Movement, Religious Education Movement were some such movements in which the demand for integration of education and religion was asserted. The world has witnessed the evil effects of materalism. Hence, it has rightly realised that humanity cannot be saved without relating education to religion. Now, the need for education integrated with religion is being felt throughout the world. Some bureaucrates and economic groups do not think it proper to give a place to religion in education. In fact, if religion is treated as 'human religion' a revolution can be brought out in the improvement of education. Peace can be established in the world through a religion integrated education based on thinking of universal peace, universal-brotherhood and universal-good.

Cautions in the Teaching of Religion

An evaluation of advantages and limitations of religious education leads us to be conclusion that religion should be given a place in education. But religion should be included in such a way that the above mentioned defects religious education may be avoided. One of the objectives of religious education is self-realisation and to inspite virtuous conduct. It is necessary to make efforts in this direction. Self-realisation and virtuous conduct are inner-impulses. They can not be imposed on anyone. Sermons and instructions alone will not achieve religious aims. Moral development and virtuous conduct through religion is possible only when opportunities are provided for such behaviour. A religious atmosphere in schools can make it possible. The incidents are greatly influenced by the ideal behaviour of teachers. So the teachers themselves should present examples of ideal behaviour by leading a religious, moral and virtuous life. The teacher religion alone cannot create a religious atmosphere in schools. All teachers should co-operate in this process.

Religious education should be kept away from narrow mindedness. It will be better to give religious eduction based on logic, analysis and criticism, otherwise it may lead to superstitions fanatics, jealousy and narrow-mentality.

In schools, religion should not be taken as an end in itself. It is simply a means for all-round development of the individual. The schools are not to be made temples, mosques, or churches by titling religious education to a particular sect. Schools are not to fulfil the functions of religious institutions other the religious institutions should work as schools. If religious institutions make an attempt for the all-round development of children through spiritual development, they will certainly lessen the burden of schools. It is, therefore, necessary for the religious bodies to take the form of educational obligations to the extent possible.

Educational Functions of Religion

A man is attracted towards religion only when he is mentally, healthy and a sound mind are sides in a sound body. So it is the function of religion to co-operate in the physical development of children. In vedic religions behaviour the ideal of celibacy is for the sake of physical development. The child who observes restraint up to maturity and takes physical exercises for the development of body makes himself sturdy. This restorative power prepares him for household life and his regulated behaviour keeps him healthy till death. Some religious people think that good physical health creates a liking or worldly pleasures and happiness. So a person desirous of religious knowledge should not pay any attention to physical development. This is their fanaticise. Religion should first of all educate the individual for his physical and mental development. Body, mind and senses are means of inhibiting religion.

Religion should always mean performing of duties. To think only of the next world (Parlok) through religious knowledge and to forget this world (Ih-lok) is not fair. The first field of performing duties is this world *Karma-Kshetra* (the field of action) is another name for *Dham-Kshetra* (fields of religious). The man who succeeds in the *Karma-Kshetra* of this world is entitled to reach the other world (Parlok). Therefore, religion should prepare man for the *Karma-Kshetra* (field of action). The field of action of the individual is determined on the basis of his aptitudes. So religion should inculcate in the child the ability to choose his field according to his interest, aptitude and to get success engaging himself in it.

The basis of religion is knowledge. An ignorant person can not be religious. A person may be familiar with religion and religious behaviour after he has attained knowledge. The basis of religion are logic, analysis, observation, contemplation and freedom of thought. So the child should be provided opportunities for independent thinking, logic, meditation, analysis and observation with an open mind. The doubt of some persons that the child does not believe in religious facts on the basis of arguments, analysis, observation etc. is baseless. The permanent religious feeling is always based on perception. To have faith in religion without independent thinking, logic and analysis will be blind-faith and fanaticism. Some people consider aesthetic sense and artistic sense as hinderance to religion. But this is not true. *Satyam, Shivam, Sundaram* (Truth, Bliss and Beautiful) and the bases for artistic and aesthetic senses. *Satyam* and *Shivam* are the bases of religion. A thing which is not true or for happiness cannot be beautiful. The carving of Jain idols in Ellora caves and Jatak stories connected with the life of Lord Buddha and their carving in Ajanta, the poetry of Sur, Tulsi and Mira and all considered unique for propagation of religious feelings. So religion should diffuse an aesthetic sense also.

Although it is true function of schools to develop the moral and character of the child, but religious institutions can bring about better moral and character development, if they pay attention in this direction. The very meaning of religion is to inspire virtuous conduct and virtuous conduct develops moral and ethical qualities. Today the country needs able and noble citizens. The religious institutions can fulfil their national duties by giving education virtuous conduct.

Arguments in Favour and Aganist Religious Education

Those who want to separate religion and education, argue in the following way:

1. To give place to religion in education is not practicable, because children of all religions come to receive education in schools. In such a situation which religion is to be taught in a school? If one particular religion is taught in the school, the followers of other religions will not accept this position. It will lead to mutual ill-will quarrel and disturbance.

2. Religion education is generally based on preaching. So long as desired changes are not brought about in the environment and ideal examples are not presented till then good conduct cannot be spread through religious education. Hence mere teaching of religious doctrines in schools will not achieve the goal of education.

4. It is not possible for the modern teacher to analyse religious knowledge dispassionately because he may be faithful only to one particular religion. Consequently, the students will be incapable of understanding the true and obscure meaning of religion. It willl be better to analyse religion with the help of science but the teachers will not accept it because science may injure the personal beliefs. In fact, it will be difficult to get able and suitable teachers for religious education. It is a difficult task to correlate education and true human religion. Every teacher may not be capable of this.

4. Doubts and mental conflicts are created in children as they cannot understand the abstract processes of sin virtue,

reward and punishment as explained in religious educational schools.

5. Religious education emphasises, religious sermons and religious knowledge. But life is not conducted according to these sermons. Man cannot become virtuous simply by getting knowledge of religion. He become virtuous only when he puts the same into practice. This is not done in schools.

6. Man imbibes 'religion' through self-realisation. Self-realisation is individualistic. Hence inclusion of personal elements in religious conduct is natural. In the school environment, collective and social tendencies are found. So personal view point of religion cannot be given importance. This view point may be suitable to those children who agree with that line of thinking but not to others who follow other view point.

7. We have already observed that religion means qualities should be developed. But history bears testimony to the fact that humanity has been oppressed in the name of religion and in place of love, compassion, sympathy and co-operation, the feelings of enmity, hatred, jealously and opposition have grown. Such examples in the history of religion may create irreligious feelings in children.

Argument in Favour of Religious Education. There may be some strength in the above arguments. But this strength will be there only to the extent to which education is imparted on the basis one particular religions without understanding the true meaning of religion. Religion is universal, omnipresent and eternal. It is necessary to present its universal form. The following arguments may be presented in favour of religious education:

1. "All-round development of man is not possible only through physical, mental and intellectual development, as requires, spiritual development also. Physical comforts alone

do not provide real pleasure and peace. The more a man is absorbed in wordly pleasures, the more he is attached towards them. He tries to get the physical comforts of this material world through all possible means (even though in human action). He becomes prepared to commit atrocities and cruel actions. This disturbs world peace. For spiritual development religion oriented education is needed. Only then the goal of an all-round development of the individual may be achieved.

2. Lack of religious faith in man is the cause of his troubles. All the vices of the world are due to ir-religiousness and materialistic tendencies. Selfishness is the outcome of materialism which creates vices like enmity, jealousy and intolerance. Hence, religious education is necessary in order to get rid of inhuman tendencies.

3. The aim of education is all-round development of the individual in which development of character is the main aim. Religious education is the best source for character development. Today education being devoid of religion, the character of many of our youths is not what it should be. Evidently, religion is to be given due place in education for the sake of character development.

4. We have said earlier that religious education becomes defective only when religion is teated in its narrow form. Religion is not be identified with any sect or opinion. The essence of all sects, is the true religion. This religion alone can be named as human religion. If it is taught through education, the follower of any religion will not be ignored. It will be worthwhile to provide education in high human ideals which are adored by people of every religion instead of giving place to the rituals of different sects.

❒

4

Primary Education

Though the missionaries had come to India with the sole purpose of trade, yet they took a very keen interest in the education of the natives of this country. They established mission centres in different parts of the country and attached elementary schools to those centres. No doubt, they carried on educational activities in this country, but the essential feature of their schools was to teach the principles of Christianity. They carried on conversion work through these institutions which served as nucleus. In spite of this, they laid out a good system of primary education in India.

Some of the important features of missionary attempts are given ahead:

(a) Religious instruction formed an integral part of general education. This, of course, created bad feelings among the people.

(b) English was introduced but most of the teachings was done through the languages of the people.

(c) The printed text books were made use of. Curriculum was broad based so as to include grammar, history and geography.

(d) Classes were conducted regularly. Teaching was made more efficient than before. A regular class system was introduced.

The missionaries worked with great zeal and enthusiasm and the schools run by them functioned well. They had sufficient funds. The indigenous schools could not compete with them and as such many of them met with a natural death. The beginning of the present system of education in India can be ascribed to the efforts of the Christian missionary schools. No doubt they introduced a new educational system in India.

Efforts of East India Company. The attitude of the company remained recalcitrant for some time. The company was authorized in 1813 to spend one lakh of rupees yearly on education. But it did not spend a penny up to 1823. As a matter of fact, rupees ten lakhs should have been spent during these ten years. In 1821, the British Parliament directed the company to accept responsibility for the education of the people, but nothing was done. In 1823, the annual grant on education was raised to ten lakhs, even then no attention was paid. It was considered that the General Committee of Public Instruction (G.C.P.I.) did not have enough funds to undertake the education of the people. In 1831, this committee, however, gave financial help to nine vernacular schools in the rural area of Saugar. This may be regarded as the first step taken by the company towards education. Obviously the company was never interested in education.

Macaulay's Minutes of 1835 did not deal with the education of the masses. The downward filtration theory failed miserably. With the adoption of English as the medium of instruction vernacular schools received a great set back. The result was that by 1852 only 30 vernacular schools survived while others languished. However some activity was witnessed in Bombay, Bengal and Madras. The private enterprise showed enthusiasm in setting up new primary schools. To quote only a few examples such an enthusiasm is evident from the efforts of Bombay. Native Education Society, which alone opened 115 primary schools. These primary schools aimed at imparting western knowledge through the medium of mother tongue. Similarly in Madras, some 70 primary schools were opened through the efforts of Sir Thomas Munro, the then Governor of Madras in 1830.

Wood's Despatch of 1854. The findings of this body with regard to the prevailing conditions of primary education in the country were discouraging. The recommendations of the Despatch were most comprehensive, which if implemented in full would have achieved excellent results. But unfortunately these remained unheeded. The suggestions given to improve primary education are given below:

(*a*) By improving the existing indigenoue schools through grant-in-aid system. These schools were considered as the very arteries through which education would flow to the masses.

(*b*) By encouraging private enterprise through liberal monetary aid.

(*c*) By opening schools by the Government according to some set plan like the Halqa Bandi System.

There is no doubt that Wood's Despatch laid the real foundation of primary education in India but there was no immediate benefit of this Despatch. The grant-in-aid system was too rigid. It did not allow any flexibility. It was like an iron jacket.

Indian Education Commission of 1802 (Hunter Commission). This commission was appointed with the chief object of reviewing the condition of Primary education and suggesting measures for its expansion. The commission also set at rest the controversy of (Should primary education be entirely provided by the government? Should the government take the help of the existing indigenous schools and private enterprises?) The Commission decided that all the primary schools owned by the government should be transferred to the local bodies, Municipal Committees and District Boards. These local bodies were required to set aside definite funds for primary education and the government was asked to help them financially to the extent of one half or at least one third of their total expenditure on primary education.

It was also decided that primary education should be given through vernacular. Indigenous schools should be duly encouraged. Arrangements for the training of primary school teachers should be made. Despite all this, primary education did not make much progress. The local bodies were inexperienced and also in their infancy, yet these could not deal with this vital problem efficiently. Even the government expenditure on primary education did not increase much.

Lord Stanley's Despatch of 1859. Finding the grant-in-aid system inflexible and as such ineffective, Lord Stanley advised that primary education should be provided by government alone. She could not absolve herself of this duty. He, therefore, suggested the levy of ' local rate' on land revenue in the rural area and houses in the urban area in all the provinces. The income thus obtained was to be spent on primary education.

Lord Curzon's Resolution of 1904. Lord Curzon was deeply interested in Indian education. No doubt, in higher education he advocated qualitative improvement, but in primary education he desired both expansion and improvement. In 1905, Lord Curzon gave a recurring grant of Rs. 35 lakhs to each of the provincial governments for helping the local bodies and private agencies engaged in providing primary education. He also recommended training for teachers, simple curriculum, grants-in-aid on the basis of efficiency and making mother-tongue as the vehicle of imparting instructions in all the primary schools. All these things resulted in the increase of both schools and pupils. Differentiation in the curriculum of the rural and urban schools was made, as their needs were different. His approach was realistic. Number of schools and scholars increased considerably. Despite all these efforts, nothing spectacular could be achieved. It merely touched the fringe of the problem. The progress was by no means rapid—it was fairly slow and halting. Indians, too were not satisfied with this little progress. They wanted free and compulsory education.

PRIMARY EDUCATION IN INDIA FROM ABOUT 1904 TO 1947

Primary Education from 1904 to 1947

The extension and improvement of primary education had been accepted in principle according to the Government's Resolution of 1904. Moreover, there was a growing feeling for the introduction of compulsory primary education amongst the masses. In this respect as small state Baroda gave the lead by enforcing compulsory primary education through an Act of 1906. It was quite successful. In 1910 Mr. G.K. Gokhale, a member of the Imperial Legislature moved a resolution in the council urging the government to make primary education free and compulsory. He also proposed that a mixed commission of officials and non-officials be appointed soon to chalk out a plan for free and compulsory education. The bill was opposed by all official and some of the non-official members, and ultimately defeated by a large number of votes—the position being 38 to 13 votes. This did not deter him and again in 1911 he did the same but this time it was turned down. There is, no doubt that Mr. Gokhale failed in his noble mission but the seeds sown by him came up quickly for harvest. The attitude of the Government underwent a change and this was no mean achievement.

Between 1910 and 1917 there was a great expansion in the private field and even the government efforts were encouraging. According to Mr. Sen, "his bill created a flutter in the dove-cots of the British Parliament." The Under

Secretary of State for India admitted the need for paying greater attention to Indian Education. In the words of Prof. Mukerji, "The official machinery of education as a result of this began to work a bit faster. Gokhale's attempts tended to focus public attention on education in general and on compulsory education in particular." What Gokhale failed to achieve in 1910-11, became a reality between 1918 and 1920, when several provincial governments made laws and passed acts for introducing compulsory education. Bombay was the first State (after Baroda's Compulsory Primary Act of 1906) to pass an Act on Compulsory Primary Education in the State. In Punjab the first primary education Act was passed in 1919.

Primary Education from 1921 to 1937

In 1921, the dyarchical type of government was established In the provinces and along with it education was declared a transferred subject. Naturally this necessitated the appointment of a Minister for Education in each province. This motivated the public interest in education. The Government and the local bodies increased their share of expenditure on primary education. The period under discussion witnessed good expansion, as would be clear from the following figures:

	1921-22	1936-37
[Govt. expenditure	902 lakhs	1236 lakhs
Local Bodies expenditure	2471akhs	438 lakhs]

Besides this, there was a great increase in the number of scholars as well.

The Hartog Committee which was appointed in 1929 to review the Primary education criticised the vast increase in number of the Primary schools and also pointed out the wastage and stagnation that had set in education. Nearly seventy five percent of the students admitted to the primary schools never reached the fourth class. This amounted to wastage of human resources. The committee consequently recommended improvement in quality rather than in quantity. It also recommended a curriculum to relate to the lives of the pupils. It considered the conditions of teachers, their training, status and other facilities to be offered to them. It also aimed at the professional growth of the teachers by providing them with refresher courses.

Provincial Autonomy and Primary Education

In 1937 Provincial autonomy was granted and the Congress was able to set up ministeries in seven provinces out of eleven, North-West Frontier Province (a land of the Pathans) being one of them. It was a commendable achievement of the Indian National Congress. It was during this period that Mahatma Gandhi gave the concept of basic education. This was given a fair trial in the seven provinces. But the autonomy was not destined to last long when, at last, war broke out in 1939. This shattered all the dreams of Gandhiji. These popular ministries decided to resign in 1939. During this short period of two years, additional grants to local bodies were given for opening new schools both for boys and girls. A training school was set up at Wardha in order to train teachers in Basic Education. About 100 Vidya Mandirs were started on these lines. These were mostly single teacher schools. In 1939, there were as many as 10 Government Basic Training Institutions and it is premised that had the war not intervened, the pattern of education would have been altogether different from what it is today.

Plan for Post-War Educational Development (Sargent Plan)

In 1945, the 'CABE' (Central Advisory Board of Education) submitted a plan for post-war educational development which is known as Sargent Plan also. Its main provisions were:

(i) Universal, free and compulsory Primary education.

(ii) Adoption of Basic Education as a national system of education.

(iii) Arrangements for teachers' training.

(iv) Need for Pre-primary education.

(v) Improvements of conditions of service of teachers.

(vi) Re-organisation of the educational system.

Unfortunately when Sargent Plan was under the active consideration of the government, the partition of the country took place. By 1947 there were nearly 1,68,000 primary schools in India with almost 1,30,28,000 students studying in them. The annual expenditure on primary education during 1946-47 (Pre-partition) period was to the tune of 14 crores of rupees. The post-independence period was considered, a period of hope.

Growth of Primary Education in India Since Independence

The Post-Independence period presented many problems like the political, social, economic and constitutional. On the eve of independence, there was nearly 17% literacy in the country. Besides this problem of mass education, reorganisation of higher education stared the government in the face. These problems were recognised as national and not provincial problems.

In 1948, an All India Education Conference was called Maulana Azad, the first Union Minister of Education which was attended by the Vice-Chancellors of Indian Universities as well as by educationists of repute. At this conference, Basic Education was adopted as the national system of education throughout the country. According to this scheme, universal free and compulsory primary education was at first to be enforced for the children between the age of 6 and 10 and afterwards its scope was to be extended for the children between the age of 11 and 14. The education of the children between the age of 6 and 10 was to be termed as Junior Basic stage while that of 11 and 14 Senior Basic stage.

Consequently a National Institute of Basic Education and a Standing Basic Education Committee were set up to help the development and expansion of basic education in the country. The Central Government immediately recommended to the states to change over to basic system of education. In order to help them in the implementation of the scheme help to the extent of 30% of their total expenditure on primary education was assured in the year 1949-50. This was done by almost all the states and some of these even enforced compulsion. Practically all the primary schools, since then, have been converted to basic pattern and curriculum has been reoriented to suit new conditions. In spite or this, the rate of progress fell from the anticipated target. The enrolment, too is discouraging. This is so because the goveniment had to face difficulties. Those are briefly as under:

(a) Lack of adequate trained teachers.

(b) Lack of funds to meet the colossal problems.

(c) Lack of faith of the people in Basic Education.

(d) Change-over is always slow.

(e) Lack of suitable buildings.

With a view to face these problems squarely a conference of the Education Ministers of the Central and State Governments was called in Delhi in 1959. It suggested the following measures to reconstruct education on the lines of basic education:

1. Basic Education Boards should be set up to secure public co-operation and advise the education departments as and when needed.

2. Conversion of teachers' training schools and college into basic type should be completed before the expiry of the Second Five Year Plan *i.e.* by 1961.

3. The integrated course of eight years (of basic education) should be developed immediately. The Junior Basic Schools should serve as feeder of Senior Basic Schools.

4. All those elementary schools which could not be converted into basic pattern, should include important features of the basic education, in order to facilitate easy conversion.

5. The standard of education in post-basic schools should be as high or even higher than that in secondary schools. These should be given due recognition by the universities.

6. Due provision be made for the further education of children after passing out of Senior Basic Schools either in Post Basic or in Secondary Schools.

Achievements in the Field of Primary Education

(a) Quite a large number of primary schools have been opened in order to reduce illiteracy under the various five-year plans.

(b) The number of scholars has also increased considerably.

(c) The rural areas, too, have been provided with a substantial number at primary schools and places which had no school formerly have a place on the education map now-a-days.

(d) Awareness amongst the masses has been created and the parents are not now prepared to get assistance from their children to supplement their incomes.

(*e*) Expenditure on Primary education since independence has increased.

(*f*) The government have subscribed liberally for providing necessary equipment and teaching aids.

(*g*) Due to financial stringency, the government have not been able to construct school buildings to meet the growing demand and have since 1956, recommended the system of double shift. In the rural areas, ordinary hutting arrangements are being utilised.

(*h*) Facilities for training and re-training of teachers have been sufficiently enlarged.

(*i*) Financial assistance to children belonging to backward classes and areas has been given.

(*j*) The curricula have been overhauled in view of the interests and needs of the children.

The above statements show that primary education after independence has made tremendous progress both in quality and quantity but still much needs to be achieved. The task is colossal and requires Herculean efforts.

Problems of Primary Education

The large scale expansion of primary education has posed many serious problems. Some of them are discussed as under :

1. Element of Wastage. Another problem arising out of rapid expansion is the resultant wastage. In India about 40% of the total enrolment in dasses one to five is in class I alone. The wastage in class I is more than half the wastage at the primary stage. If more than half of the entire children entering the bottom class of the schools waste away, it will mean both education and administrative wastage of such a high nature that its implications have caused concern.

2. Enrolment Problems. The demand for education has increased so much that it is getting well-nigh impossible to secure admissions to schools. This is true of big places like Delhi, Bombay, Calcutta, Madras, Kanpur etc. The result is that many unrecognised schools charging too high fees have cropped up.

3. Shortage of Trained Teachers. In the Third Five Year Plan, it was decided that the percentage of trained teachers will be raised to 75%. But unfortunately this target has not been touched. There has therefore, been no corresponding increase in teacher training facilities. Quite a large number of primary schools are without trained teachers.

4. Primary Education Most Unpsychological. Primary education is not based on the psychology of the child and the methods adopted are unpsychological. The same age-old technique of teaching is in vogue. Cramming is encouraged. It is too bookish and does not train the senses of the children. It deals more with books and less with tools. Moral education is conspicuous by its absence.

5. Absence of Model Primary Schools. The working of the primary schools is rigid and formal. A few model schools in every important place need to be opened so as to serve as models. Such schools should serve as a vanguard to other institutions.

6. Single Teacher Schools. These present great difficulties. A single teacher cannot efficiently handle all the four classes especially when the strength of the pupils is too high. Individual attention which is essential at this stage, cannot be given.

7. Primary Schools—Weakest Link. Primary education is the very basis of higher education. If the foundation is not well built up, the super-structure would remain weak. Some have boldly remarked that "Primary education is the weakest link in the educational chain." It needs to be strengthened. The total educational expenses devoted to primary schools are much less than those devoted to secondary and university education. These schools are over-crowded, have inadequate accommodation, equipment and teachers. The local bodies are inefficient bodies to run these schools well. In fact in any programme of national development all stages are equally important.

8. Lack of Interest of the Private Agencies. With the introduction of the grant-in-aid system, it was expected that private enterprise would enter the field. Since primary schools cost more than they yield as income, private agencies have not considered it worthwhile to take up the responsibility.

9. Lack of Proper Supervision. The education department has failed miserably to exercise proper control over these institutions. The primary schools need better supervision as these serve as the first door through which the children reach the threshold of knowledge.

Suggestions

1. Freedom of mind is most important as without it there can be no other freedom and progress. So the Primary stage must be revitalised.

2. Primary education needs better attention than has been given so far to it. In fact the foundation should be well laid and funds should not hinder its progress. No doubt that defence and development are very important but education of the children is no less vital. K. G. Saiyidain has aptly remarked, "Human resources need more attention and as such no amount is too big for their development."

3. The quality of teaching should be improved so as to avoid wastage. The teacher must be adequately trained for

this job, because handling of youngsters is not an easy job. The teacher, as a matter of fact, must be humane in his attitude and must proceed, on the assumption that in every child, there is some spark of talent, of intelligence, of goodness, which a primary teacher must try to discover.

4. The teachers' salaries should be sufficiently increased so that no economic problems upset them. "In fact in selecting teachers and determining their conditions of service, pay-masters need to realise that they are not buying commercial junk for which they would like to pay the lowest price but choosing persons in whose keeping they propose to entrust the future of their children and country." - K.G. Saiyidain.

5. **Teachers' Training.** Training of teachers for rural schools should be agriculture-oriented so as to relate instruction to their real lives. At present it is divorced from it.

6. **Need for Good Curriculum.** The curriculum should not be wooden and rigid. It should be flexible and formulated in accordance with the needs of the particular locality.

7. **In-Service Training.** Arrangement for the in-service training of such teachers should be made from time to time in order to make them conversant with the latest trends in education.

8. **Emphasis on Moral Training.** Moral instruction should form a part of the primary education curriculum. The teacher should give much greater time and attention to the formation of character and personality and the cultivation of right attitudes and values than to the pouring of knowledge.

9. **Education to be Joint Venture.** Education should be considered as a joint venture. It is not the teacher alone who is held responsible for it. It has to be a comradeship all along the line between the inspectors and the teachers, the teachers and the children, the teachers and the parents. They are all engaged in a great human endeavour, to build a finer type of

great human being and, through him, a more gracious social order. It is, therefore, essential that all these partners in a great enterprise take one another into confidence. The respect to the teacher must be given importance over other things.

10. **Need for Social Education.** Social education should receive encouragement as it will create consciousness amongst the illiterate masses. Importance of education can be realised better by educated parents.

Objectives of Primary Education

The objectives of primary education are as follows :

(a) To give an adequate mastery over the basic tools of learning.

(b) To prepare children for good citizenship, to develop in them a love for their country, its traditions and culture and to inspire in them a sense of service and loyalty.

(c) To develop international understanding and the spirit of universal brotherhood.

(d) To inculcate in them a better attitude towards life.

(e) To bring about a harmonious development of the child's personality, by providing for his physical, intellectual, social, emotional and moral needs.

(f) To prepare children for life through the provision of worth while practical activities and experiences.

In spite of the fact that compulsory primary education acts have been passed in the country, the dream of free and compulsory primary education has not been realised as yet. The problems are given as under :

1. Employment of Children on Petty Jobs. The parents in the hope of securing some material gain, prefer them to take up petty jobs. The clause 10 of the Punjab Primary Education Act 1960 forbids the children between 6 and 11 years to pick up a job. Both the employer and the employee are considered as offenders and are liable to be prosecuted. Yet the beauty is that this clause is being observed more in its breach rather than in its observance. Strict observance is needed.

2. Poverty. The general poverty of the people of this country is proverbial. There are innumerable people who can hardly eke out their existence. The parents cannot possibly afford to send their children to schools. Instead they are a source of income. The children pick up certain petty jobs or assist their parents in their occupations. To escape legislation, the parents play tricks with the attendance authorities and very often they succeed. Some of the parents are backward and as such do not have faith in the education of their children.

3. Lack of Exemplary Punishments. The authorities concerned with such an education fail to exercise their powers properly. The punishments given are too mild. Generally the defaulters are dealt by block education officers who are easily accessible. As a matter of fact, such cases must be tried by Magistrates as laid down by the rules. In the absence of good punishment, cumpulsory legislation is meaningless. The defaulters are left off by ordinary fines.

4. Lack of Propaganda. The government and other educational agencies must bring home to the masses about the usefulness of education. This can be done through lectures and screening of films. A general awareness must be created amongst the people.

5. Attitude of Parents. Majority of the parents do not believe in the usefulness of education. They feel that their children will be lost to their profession. This apathy on the parent's part is not conducive to the development of the children.

6. Fictitious Enrolments. Allured by bribery or certain other advantages, the teachers indulge in fictitious enrolment. They keep records of the students in absentia. This malpractice is too common and should be checked by the authorities.

7. Dearth of Teachers and Adequate Equipment. Universal, free and compulsory education would need a large number of teachers and up-to-date equipment. Shortage of teachers and dearth of adequate equipment generally results in inefficient teaching and indiscipline.

8. Wrong Delegation of Powers. The teachers have been given powers to deal with the recalcitrant parents for not sending their children to the schools. The status of the primary teacher being insignificant in the eyes of the villagers, he is unable to make full use of his powers. Very often he yields either to the temptation or pressures of the people. He is, therefore, ineffective in this.

9. Lack of Facilities for Poor Children. There is hardly any provision of helping the poor children with suitable stipends or free books and other reading material.

Recommendations of Kothari Commission

The recommendations of Kothari Commission on primary education have been discussed under four heads :

1. Expansion of Primary Education. Primary education should be given free and on a compulsory basis.

The Commission recommends that five years of good and effective education should be provided to all children by 1975-76 and that seven years of such education should be given by 1985-86. It also suggests that emphasis should be laid on the reduction of wastage and stagnation. It should be seen that not less than 80 percent of the children that enter class I reach class VII in the period of seven years.

Children who are not yet 14 years old at the end of class VII should be retained in the school upto 14 years and provided with special vocational courses of their choice. In order to implement all this the Commission recommends that each state and district should be required to prepare a respective plan for the development of primary education in its locality for achieving the above mentioned targets.

2. Universal Enrolment. A system of pre-registration should be introduced. The bulk of the students in this class should consist of children in the age-group of 5-6 or 6-7.

More the transfer rate of students from the end of the lower primary stage to the higher primary, which is at present about 80 percent, should be raised to 100 percent by the end of the 5th plan.

In this way universal enrolment would be secured.

3. Universal Provision of Schools. The expansion of primary schools should be so planned that a lower primary school is available within a distance of nearly a mile from the place of every child and a higher primary school be within one to three miles from the place of every child. In this way primary education can be made more effective and universal.

4. Universality of Retention. The quality of primary education needs to be improved and stagnation reduced. The target should be to reduce stagnation and wastage by about half by 1976 and to eliminate them by 1986.

The Commission further recommends that stagnation and wastage in other classes should be reduced by providing part time education, by improving schools and by a more vigorous programme of social education.

Brief Report of the Committee of Members of Parliament (1967)

(1) It was realised by the Committee of Members of Parliament on Education that good and effective primary education, on a free and compulsory basis, is the corner-stone of democracy. It is to be given top priority and should be undertaken in two stages given as under :

(i) Universal education should be provided for all children upto the age of 11 years. This will constitute the first stage.

(ii) In the second stage, this age limit should be increased to 14 years.

(2) Efforts should be made to avoid wastage and stagnation and and it should be seen that every child enrolled in schools passes regularly from one class to another till he completes the primary stage. In other words no failures should take place.

(3) The under-developed areas be given more attention in the form of financial help by the State and the Central Governments. This will remove the disparities in education.

(4) Primary education, being the birth right of every child in the country, should be made free immediately. In fact a primary school should be within an easy reach of every child of this age.

The report further suggests that all this can be achieved through the co-operation of the people and also by following the programme given as under:

(a) **Proper Arrangement for Pre-Primary Education.** This will prepare the children for compulsory schooling.

(b) Quality of teaching at the primary level be sufficiently raised. For this purpose trained and efficient staff

shall have to be appointed and the number of single-teacher schools shall have to be reduced.

(c) Facilities should exist for part-time primary education to accommodate those children who are unable to attend regular schools.

(d) Classes I and II be considered as one integrated unit. It is also called ungraded system.

Fulfilment of the Constitutional Directive

The Constitutional Directive required every state to strive to provide free and compulsory education for all children upto the age of 14 years and an all-out efforts was made to achieve the target by 1960. The task was colossal. The path was strewn with difficulties. The strenuous efforts that the states and the centre expended on the cause for which Gokhale once fought tooth and nail could not bear fruit as desired. The following were the difficulties that adequate progress:

1. Lack of adequate resources.
2. A momentous increase in population.
3. An opposition to the education of girls.
4. A large number of children of the backward classes.
5. General poverty of the masses.
6. Their illiteracy and indifference.

The financial resources with the country were being diverted to improve national economy. The task of educating the ever growing student population of the age group 6-14 free of cost was colossal and complex. The population of India in 1960 was about 500 million, and half of it was below 18 and it was expected that more than 5 million would be added to the student population every year. The general poverty of the masses and their illiteracy and indifference and their apathy to educate their daughters did not let us achieve the targets. The Government of India expressed in 1964 its grave concern at its not being able to provide free and universal education for all children upto 14 years of age. The public was snsisting persistently on fixing an early deadline for the fulfilment of the Constitutional Directive when the Education Commission was appointed in 1964.

The Commission recommended that free and compulsory education for all children upto the age of 14 could be provided if each state took the three following practical measures:

Universal Provision of School Facilities. Every child has to be provided a school within his reach. By the end of the third plan every child living in a village with a population of 300 or over was provided with schooling facility for his primary education. But the provision of a school within easy distance from the home of every child attending a middle school could not be made by that time in many states. As a middle school cannot be set-up on financial reasons in every village, it will have to be shared by a group of small villages; so a middle school should be so planned that it may be one to three miles from the home of the child.

Universal Enrolment. The problem of universal enrolment appears to be rather difficult. We will have to start a system of pre-registration for all fresh admissions to class I. We will have to make it legally obligatory for all parents to get their children admitted into class I at 6+. We will have to mobilise the teaching community to take an annual census of all children whose age is 5+ and prepare admission plans. In large cities such a procedure of pre-registration and pre-census-talking may be difficult. In the initial stages we will have to admit all the over-age boys and girls but later this difficulty will disappear.

The problem of universal admission into and enrolment in class V. Not all boys and girls who are reading in class IV move up to class V. There are two reasons. The higher primary school is either far away from the home of the child or the parent is indifferent to the education of the child and wants him/her to enter the world of work. The difficulty can be surmounted by planning higher primary schools in such a way that each child can move to it easily and by persuading parents and telling them the utility of education and the inevitability of mixed schools.

Universal Retention. The problem of universal retention, when the two problems of universal provision and enrolment have been solved, appears to be easy, because it is within the reach of every school. When once a child is admitted to class I, it is the responsibility of school people to see that the child progress regularly from year to year, and to make the school environment so attractive that the child does not leave it. It means that there is neither stagnation nor wastage in the primary education.

The Present State of Universalising Free and Compulsory Primary Education. The country is alive to the promise it had made because an all-out effort has been made after 1966 to achieve the Constitntional Directives. Today more than 7 crores of children are attending schools. This number represents 85% of the total population in age group 6-11 as compared to 33%, three decades ago. The Primary Education is free in all the states and it is compulsory in most of the states. It is free in class I to V in all government schools and schools sum by local bodies in every state. It is also free in classes VI to VIII in all states except for boys in Orissa, Uttar Pradesh and West Bengal. The primary education is compulsory in all states except Bihar, Manipur, Meghalaya, Nagaland, Sikkim and Tripura where the states have not been able as yet to exact legislation for compulsory education. In most of the union territories *e.g.* Delhi, Andman and Nicobar Islands and Chandigarh there is such legislation for compulsory education.

At the beginning of the sixth Five Year Plan, the strategy has been to make primary education universal. It does not mean that the country is not making serious attempts to universalise Middle School Education from class V to VII or from VI to VIII in the age group 11-14. It is in the sixth plan (1978-83) that the country has taken very serious steps to universalise elementary education within a period of ten years, The states are trying to cover about half of the total enrolled and drop-out children with the help of giving this section of children non-formal part-time education. The backwards are given in this Plan a financial help of Rs. 25 crores because it is, in these states that we have the greatest number of children not enrolled in the age group 11-14.

Wastage and Stagnation in Primary Education

It is a fact that the child who is enrolled in class I does not progress regularly from year to year. In one class or the other he fails and has to repeat the same class. There is stagnation (in moving up). He may have to repeat a class once and sometimes twice also. There is yet another distressing aspect of school education. The child who gets admission to a school leaves the school before he compelets the prescribed age or class. He drops out. There is wastage. The child may drop out because of economic reasons. He may drop out because he does not find school curriculum to his taste.

A large number of pupils either have to repeat a class once or twice or have to discontinue their education. The amount of wastage and stagnation in our system of education is too much. The evil was first brought to light by the Hartog Committee in 1929. Since then much work has been done in finding out the extent of stagnation and wastage but little effort has been made to reduce it.

The Hartog Committee defined wastage as the premature withdrawal of children from school at any stage before the completion of the course. There is one difficulty in accepting the above definition. Should all pupils who drop out before passing the last class of a stage be treated as cases of wastage? In our definition we have used the word 'till'. If a child does not leave the school till he completes the prescribed class or age, he is a case of wastage.

Some thinkers relate the phenomenon of wastage to the objectives of education. For example, if we take one of the objectives of primary education as the attainment of permanent literacy, then any child who drops out or is withdrawn from the school before achieving the desired goal, he is a case of wastage.

How to Measure the Extent of Wastage? A number of methods have been suggested to measure the extent of wastage at any stage of education. These methods are :

(a) H. Sharp's method.

(b) Hartog Committee's method.

(c) The method of Increment of Gains.

(d) The movement of Pupils method.

We shall explain only two methods. The most plausible method of finding out the extent of wastage in any stage is to follow the movement of a representative set of pupils from class to class through subsequent years till the last class is reached. For example, we may take a most representative group of 1000 boys or of girls who join class I in a given year, and find out the total number of pupils who leave from class I, II, III, and IV. For finding out the number of pupils who leave a certain class, say II, we will have to find out all possible cases such as the following :

(a) the number who left the school after completing class I in the first attempt and going to class II.

(*b*) the number who left the school after completing class I in the second attempt and going to class II (9-).

(*c*) the number who left the school after completing class I in the third attempt and going to class II (10-).

(*d*) the number who passed class I and II but left after failing in 11(8+).

(*e*) the number of who passed class I in two attempts and failed in class II and left (9+).

(*f*) the number who passed class I in three attempts and failed in class II (10+).

(*g*) the number who passed class I in two attempts and failed twice in II (10+).

Such a method was used by the Research unit in the Directorate of Education, Maharashtra state and the amount of wastage came to about 41% at the lower primary stage. The figures given in brackets indicate the number of years spent in the school. Such a method, though very sound, is not usable.

The most rough and ready method to measure the extent of wastage is to compare the lessening in enrolment from class to class over a number of years. This method was used by the Hartog Committee in 1929.

The following conclusions are drawn from the data which shows the extent of diminution in enrolment for the country as a whole for a period of 12 years, separately for boys and girls and for primary and middle classes.

1. The wastage is very large at the primary stage.
2. The wastage is larger for girls than for boys at each stage.
3. The wastage is greatest for class I for both sexes.

4. The wastage at the primary stage for boys is fairly constant.

5. The wastage at the primary stage for girls is decreasing.

6. The wastage at the middle school stage is decreasing for both sexes.

Measures to Reduce Wastage and Stagnation

1. Changing the Admission Policies. The highest incidence of wastage and stagnation is in class I and one of the potent reasons for this is that we keep open the admission to class I throughout the year and the child who is admitted at the fag end of the year fails and has to remain in the same class for the next year too. Tasting failure in the beginning classes has a demoralising effect on the child as well as on the parents. Hence admission should be restricted to only first three months of the academic year.

2. Introduction of Upgraded Unit and Abolition of Examinations. The main idea behind the concept of 'upgraded unit' recommended by Kothari Commission is to individualise instruction by permitting every child to progress at his own pace. The abolition of examinations and automatic promotion from one class to another is the main idea behind the concept of 'upgraded unit'.

3. Play Way Technique. The children of classes I and II need a smooth transition from the play-orientated world of infancy to the formal type of school environment. The traditional methods of teaching, and unattractive school environment scare them away. Irregular attendance results in poor achievements in studies. Failures in examinations ultimately leads to wastage. At this stage irregularity in attendance is neither due to truancy nor due to home circumstances. The children are considered to be nuisance to the family and not economically useful; so the parents are eager to send them to school so as to get rid of them at least for a few hours in the day. The children themselves run away from school or remain playing elsewhere because the school environment is not attractive. Hence playway methods of teaching may minimize the incidence of stagnation and wastage.

4. Financial Help to Parents. Parents who cannot afford to buy books and other items of stationery may be given help according to their economic status, In order that the lack of reading and writing material may not affect the achievement of children in studies book—banks may be opened so that poor and deserving students may borrow books from them.

5. Adjusting School Hours and School Vacations to Meet the Economic Needs of the Country. If the school hours and school vacations are adjusted in such a way that grown-up children of class VIII to X can assist their parents and also study at schoool, the incidence of wastage and stagnation may be minimised. In rural areas schools may be of 3 hours' duration and school vacation may be synchronised with the sowing and harvesting periods of major crops. The teachers and social workers may undertake social and economic surveys to find out the needs of the community and adjust school hours accordingly.

6. Remedial Teaching for Weak Students. Stagnation can be reduced by the provision of remedial teaching to weak students before or after the school hours or on Sundays and holidays.

7. Improving School Community Relations. Whenever a child shows signs of irregularity in attendace or truancy, it should be the sacred duty of the teacher to contact his parents without any loss of time because a mere enquiry on the part of the teacher will have a salutary effect in bringing back the child to school. School should be made a community centre and effective P.T.A. may be established.

8. Appointment of School Mothers and Women Teachers. To fight social backwardness of parents who suffer from social taboos, who have a little regard for the education of their daughters, a campaign of adult literacy may be adopted and widely spread. The apathy of parents towards girl education may be broken to some exent by appointing school mothers and women teachers in primary schools in rural areas. Women teachers for rural areas may be made available, by the introduction of short-term training courses, by the relaxation of age limit for recruitment to government service and by a provision of incentives to them in the form of special allowance for rural service.

❐

5

Basic Education System

Basic education is a double edged weapon; on the one hand it deals with the all round development of the child, and on the other and most important side it prepares the base for the development of higher education. Thus whatever satisfies our basic needs is the medium of our education. Basic Education encourages a clean, healthy and self-supporting life.

The fundamental concept of basic education is to make productive crafts the medium of education. According to Gandhiji, "With the help of craft education, man will gain health and happiness through labour; self-reliance, self-confidence and self dependence through industry; devotion to work and a scientific mind through action, orderliness and cleanliness through work; patience through corporate life; spirit of service through co-operation satisfaction of the thirst for knowledge and self study through skill in work and imaginativeness through construction."

Salient Features of Basic Education

1. Free and Compulsory Education to All. It should be free and compulsory for seven years (from seven to fourteen years). The school leaving age for children should be at least 14 years, when the child learns effective literacy and develops proper control over his senses. The education should be both intellectual and manual and should help the child to overcome adolescent age normally. Seven years free and compulsory education is emphasised for two reasons :

(a) Ours is a democratic country and success of democracy depends upon the educated and enlightened citizens.

(b) Gandhi dreamt of a classless society, free of exploitation of any kind, which can be eliminated if everyone is educated.

2. Education to Centre Round Some Craft. Gandhiji gives pivotal place to craft. It should be productive and manual. It must possess educative possibilities. Different subjects should be taught around it. Craft should not be taught separately. The whole education is to be given through it. Gandhiji says, "I would begin the child's education by teaching it a useful handicraft and enabling it to produce from the moment it begins training. I hold that the highest development of the mind and soul is possible under such a system of education." The craft must relate to the environments of the children. Apart from this, the craft sharpens the mind. Again he says, "The handicrafts are to be taught not merely for the production work but for developing the intellect of the pupils." He emphasised the economic, intellectual and moral aspects through basic education.

3. Mother Tongue as the Medium of Instruction. Gandhiji was fully conscious of the harm done by English to Indians. According to him it had created a bar between the highly educated few and the uneducated many. He goes a step further and says, "It has cast upon the educated class a burden which has maimed (crippled) them mentally for life and made them strangers in their own land." Mother-tongue, according to Gandhiji, is not only to act as the medium of instruction but also to take the first place in languages. A child can express himself well in his mother-tongue. To learn a foreign language is to become an alien in one's own land. It means waste of time, energy and money. A foreign language is a hinderance in the development of personality as it puts a check on understanding and expression. It is through mother-tongue, that the child can develop his powers of comprehension, thinking and reasoning. Gandhiji's insistence on the use of mother-tongue as medium of instruction was educationally sound. Subsequent re-thinking on it has fully supported the contention of Gandhiji and has led to the introduction of languages as medium of instruction. He was not against English study. In fact he wanted his countrymen to study English as would be clear from his remarks, "I do not want my house to be walled in on all sides and my windows to be stuffed. I want the cultures of all lands to be blown about my house as freely as possible. But I refuse to be blown off my feet by any. I would have our young men and women with literary tastes to learn as much of English and other world languages as they like, then except them to give the benefits of their learning to India and to the world. But I would not have a single Indian to forget, neglect, or be ashamed of his mother-tongue. Mine is not a religion of the prison-house."

4. Correlation. It is one of the important features and crux of basic education. It is a technique which tries to establish reciprocal relationship between the various subjects of the curriculum for the better understanding of the subject under discussion. It draws out the points of resemblance which different studies of the child at school, bear to one another. It is a wonderful device for motivating the children.

5. Self-supporting Aspect of Education. Gandhiji was aware of the poverty of the country. His dreams of universal, free and compulsory education could not be realised and as such he introduced the element of self supporting in his scheme of education. He wanted to see every citizen of the land literate. He introduced a manual productive craft, the sale of which would make education self-supporting. Gandhiji said, "An education should not be financed out of the excise revenue, neither out of land revenue. Under 'Swaraj' its main prop should be spinning wheel. If the spinning wheel and loom are in every school and college, our education would easily pay its way." Psychologically, economically and sociologically the concept is true. It does not only instil self confidence and pride in children but also prepares them for a richer life. Craft work according to Gandhiji is not merely a mean literary education, it is also an end in itself. Self-support is the acid test of its reality.

6. The Ideal of Citizenship. It is an important feature of basic education. Mr. Varkey remarks in his connection like this, "We need a system of education that will secure at least the minimum of education required for the intelligent exercise of rights, and duties of citizenship." Basic education will produce useful citizens. The scheme encourages co-operative activities and thus lays the foundations of ideal citizenship. Dr. Zakir Hussain Committee also observes in the same strain, "An education which produces drags and parasites—whether rich or poor stands condemned. Basic scheme is designed to produce workers who will look upon all kinds of useful work as honourable."

7. Child Centred Education. The child is the central figure of educational activities. The curriculum is suited to his needs and not the child to the curriculum.

The curriculum consists of the actual experiences acquired by the child through work and play. All knowledge is correlated with the activity of the child. Nothing is forced on the child from without. The development takes place from within through his own activities. The child unfolds himself through self-activity. The teacher acts only as a friend, a guide and philosopher. It is in this sense that education is child centred and not book centred as was the case in the past.

8. Relationship with Life. Education should be closely related to life. Basic education unifies knowledge and does not permit division of knowledge into water tight compartments. Correlation unifies knowledge as a whole. There are three centres of correlation—craft, physical environment and social environment and these will achieve perfect integration of curriculum.

9. The Cult of Non-Violence. Gandhiji has a strong faith in non-violence. Naturally his scheme could not remain unaffected by it. He desired to solve all the problems non-violently. "Our arithmetic, our science, our history will have a non-violent approach and the problems in these subjects will be coloured by non-violence." Gandhiji, thus conceived of education as a process that would fit a man for playing useful role in the non-violent social order. He believed in the force of love to prevail in all spheres and especially in education.

10. It is a Comprehensive Scheme. It is a scheme for all. Though the emphasis is on the elementary education, yet it covers all the stages and links the education as a whole. The stages are as follows :

(*a*) Pre-basic stage meant for children between 2-6 years.

(*b*) Basic stage covers the children between 6-14 years.

(*c*) Post basic stage caters to the higher needs of the pupils between 15-17 years.

(*d*) University stage meets the requirements of the pupils between 18-21 years.

(*e*) Social education is a part of basic education. It deals with the education of the unfortunate illiterate adults.

It is, therefore, an all-round scheme and does not leave out any stage untouched.

Gandhian Philosophy of Education

Gandhiji's philosophy of education is deep. It is based on his philosophy of life. He believed in perfect democracy which worked for the happiness of all without any distinction of caste, colour or creed. Gandhi enjoys the same position in India as Pestalozzi enjoys in Western Educational World. Both are known as the father of educational systems. Through education Gandhiji wished to bring about a revolution in the educational, social, economic and political fields. He was quite aware of the general backwardness of the people and desired to raise them in the scale of human existence. He, therefore, devised a scheme of basic education which would achieve these ends.

His Philosophy of Life

His philosophy of life determined his philosophy of education. His greatest creed is love of humanity and service of God. He says, "The only way to find God is to see Him in His creation." This implies serving God through human beings.

Secondly, he believed in non-violence. What is non-violence? It is love for all and hatred for none. Human beings should live peacefully with each other.

Thirdly, he wanted a social order which should be free from all types of exploitations. He wanted to forge a classless society, a society in which all enjoyed the same privileges and status.

The only force that people can use is moral force. He wanted liquidation of capital. He proposed to build up the economic and social structure on decentralised industry and agriculture. He recommends cottage and village industries.

He wanted to re-create society. Rejuvenation of Indian society could only take place, if village life was revived and vitalised. According to him true India lived in villages and unless their lot could be improved, Indians will remain submerged in poverty and ignorance.

As a true philosopher, he could not help being an educator for achieving his life's mission. He evolved an educational system as a dynamic side of his philosophy. By education, he means, "an all-round drawing out of the best in child and man-body, mind and spirit." It is one of the means whereby man and woman can be educated. Literacy in itself can be no education.

Like Rousseau he wished to restore the child to his right position in the scheme of education. He aimed at the harmonious development of the child. For realising his aim, he hit upon a suitable method. He says, "I would begin the child's education by teaching handicraft and enabling it to produce from the moment it begins its training." He feels that the highest development of the mind and soul could be possible under such a system of education. He did not want the children to learn the craft mechanically but scientifically. "The child should know the why and wherefore of every process."

This is the core of his philosophy of education. Manual activity is essential for educating the child. The school is not to be just a school where a vocation is added to the already existing curricula, but all subjects are to be taught through a vocation. This does not mean that the schools would be converted into production places (factories). According to him the craft has both educational and economic value. It will give confidence to the children and they shall learn and earn simultaneously. They shall be no burdens on their parents. Moreover they are being helped to be useful to the country.

His philosophy of education is centred around two things:

(*i*) That education should be woven round a suitable craft.

(ii) That the craft chosen should meet the expenses of the teacher's salaries.

Gandhiji was a realist, a born teacher and a psychologist. He was convinced that education imparted through some handicraft or industry would suit the children of this country. He made manual training as the means of literary training. This would help the children to develop certain traits of character. Character building was considered essential. Like every other great philosopher, Gandhiji tried to translate his philosophy into actual practice Basic scheme of education is the outcome of his experiments in education performed at the Phoenix Settlement and at the Tolstoy Farm in South Africa.

Conviction in Idealism, Naturalism and Pragmatism

Like Aristotle he believed in the realisation of supreme Truth, Beauty and Goodness. To him, Truth is the greatest God. This could be achieved through 'Ahimsa'.

"Ahimsa and Truth," says he, "are so inter-woven that it is practically impossible to disentangle and separate them." Ahimsa is the means, Truth is the end. So Ahimsa is our duty. He had idealism in mind in formulating his scheme of education.

Like Rousseau, he was an ardent follower of naturalism. He reveals naturalism through ideal environments and surroundings. He was against artificial environments. He advocated full freedom to the children and very much deprecated punishment. To him, natural surroundings will provide innumerable opportunities to children for self-expression.

Like Dewey, he was a thorough pragmatist Education through activity is an ideal approach. His education stresses on action rather than reflection and it lays emphasis on practice more than on theory. 'Learning by doing' is reflected in his method. He, therefore, nicely combined idealism, naturalism and pragmatism in his scheme of education.

Character Building

He laid too much stress on the character formation of the people. He therefore impressed upon them the necessity of religious education. By religious education he did not believe in certain religious dogmas, rather he meant cultivating the habit of following every religion in spirit of reverence and broad-minded tolerance. True religion would mean faith to the Divine. "It is faith that steers us through stormy seas, faith that moves mountains. Without faith this world will come to naught in a moment." He considered education as the instrument through which faith, fearlessness and a cultured life can be cultivated.

"Prayer has been the saving of my life. Without it I should have been a lunatic long ago," said he. So through religious instructions, he wishes to build the character of the children. This is how he ultimately aimed at the national character, which had gone down too low owing to defective education. To him religion was tile essence of education.

Belief in the Complete Development of Man

He believed in the harmonious development of man. This would be evident from his conception of education. "By education I mean an all-round drawing out of the best in child and man—body, mind and spirit." The personality must be well-knit. Development of the whole man was one of the aims of education as envisaged by him. "It is neither the body nor the soul we are training—it is the whole man and let us not divide him into parts." writes an American educationist. Gandhiji shares his views completely.

Self-Sufficiency of Self-Supporting Aspect

Gandhlji was fully conscious of the financial condition of the people and the country. Compulsory and free education was too great an undertaking. The Indian economy, as it then stood, could not embark on such an ambitious plan. He therefore wanted to make education self-sufficient. He had seen the educational systems of other countries and especially of Japan, where the children earned as they learnt. By making education self-supporting, there was every chance of realising the dream of his life. He evolved a plan to fulfil this ambition of undertaking the education of all school-going children in the country. He believed that any system of education based on craft would prove self-supporting. In the words of Gandhiji, "As a nation we are so backward in education that we cannot hope to fulfil our duty to the nation in this aspect in a given time during this generation, if the programme is to depend on money. If education is made free and universal, I fancy, that even under an ideal system of Govt. we shall not be able to devote crores of rupees which one should require for finding education for all the children of school going age. I have, therefore, made bold even at the risk of losing a reputation for constructive ability, to suggest that education should be self-supporting." So Gandhiji wished the child to earn from the day it began training by learning some useful craft and producing articles. He wanted every school to meet the entire expenses of children's education and some of the school expenditure. Self-supporting aspect means that child should do such an activity which enables him to have some "earning along with learning." Such an education would be useful because earning aspect would encourage the child and would not prove a burden on the parents. It would also satisfy the creative urge of the child. Apart from this, the child develops a sound mind with feeling of possession, self-confidence, initiative and belongingness. His personality becomes well adjusted.

Gandhiji, therefore conceived a system of education, known as the basic education which contributed towards self-sufficiency in education. He was a practical genius. According to him, "Self-sufficiency is not a prior condition, but to me it is the acid test." He used self-sufficiency in two senses:

(a) Such education should make a child self-sufficient in later life after completing his education in the school.

(b) It should be able to meet partly or wholly the recurring expenses of education, including the salaries of teachers. Gandhiji says, "The child at the age of 14, that is after finishing a seven years course, should be discharged as an earning unit." According to him, the term self-supporting is that the expenses of teacher's salaries, apart from children's own expenses, should be met through the manual and productive work. He has firm conviction that "every school can be made self-sufficient, the condition being the state taking over the produce of these schools." Zakir Hussain Committee has fully endorsed the self-supporting aspect but warned against some dangers arising out of it, "In the working of this scheme the economic aspect may be stressed at the sacrifice of the educative objectives. Teachers may devote most of their attention and energy to extracting the maximum amount of labour from children, while neglecting the intellectual, social and moral implications and possibilities of craft training. This point may be constantly kept in mind in the training of teachers as well as in the direction of the work of the supervisory staff and must colour all educational activity.

Correlation an Effective Method

The Basic Education System rests on correlation. It is one of the important features of basic education. Without it, education would be meaningless. In fact the success of basic education depends upon the intelligent working of correlation. "Correlation is a technique which establishes reciprocal relationship between the various subjects of the curriculum for the better understanding or the subject under discussion." It draws out the points of resemblance, which different studies of the child at school bear to one another. It is a wonderful device which can be used safely for creating interest in the lesson and thus makes learning easy. Shri Ranganathan commenting on Basic Education said, "Its distinctive pedagogic (science of teaching) method is nodal (knotty). Correlation between the crafts and various subjects is the essential land mark in each."

Correlation selects related parts and combines them into a new complex piece of information which becomes an agreeable ready made food for the growth of child's mind. In the basic scheme of education knowledge is expected in one compact whole. The basic education, therefore, is an effort to inter-relate and correlate the life of the child with his environments. The pupil's activity and his need should be integrated with the environmental life, and the different activities, whether conducted outside or in the class room, should possess a good deal of correlation among themselves. According to this conception the knowledge is not to be given in isolated units, but it should take place through an inter-linked process. The remarks of Secondary Education Commission are worth examining: "It should not stultify (undo) its educational value by being split up into a number of isolated, uncoordinated water-tight subjects."

This conception is nothing new. It is as old as the methodology of teaching. In fact the idea of correlation owes its existence to the Psychological Principle of "Apperception of Thought" first used by Herbert Spencer in teaching.

Why is Correlation Needed?

What is the philosophy behind it? There is a need for correlation because it springs from the principle of association of ideas. Knowledge has to be given as a unified whole. It cannot be given in an isolated manner. It presents the problems of life in a normal way. Education is for life and as such it cannot be divorced from currents of life. Actual problems and situations in life are never tackled by reference to one field of knowledge. It needs for its solution, the help of a number of subjects closely related. Correlation, therefore, serves as an effective method against narrow specialisation and safeguards the liberal aspect of education. It makes education more effective. It is a useful weapon in the armoury of a teacher, with the help of which he gives knowledge as an integrated one. The teacher makes it a motivating tool as well. Correlation is regarded as the soul of basic education. According to Dr. Sitaram. "When you take a lump of cotten and clear it of dirt, thrash it and card it, spin the yarn and weave the cotton, the whole range of agriculture and industry, of history and geography of economic and politics is capable of being taught—centring round the craft on hand." Zakir Hussair Committee opined that craft alone may not suffice as the medium of correlation. They suggested two more *via* media :

(a) Physical environment;

(b) Social environment.

Craft Work in Basic Education

The traditional system of education was too rigid, wooden and literary. It failed to satisfy the practical problems of the pupils life. It created unemployment on a large scale and turned out educated persons who were misfits in the changing social order. Such an education tended to produce youngman who were Indian in blood only otherwise they had developed western ways of life. They were strangers to their people. In view of this, a new system of education was urgently needed for the establishment of a new social order in the country. Gandhiji's Basic Education was to remove the glaring defects of the traditional system.

Emphasis on Craft

Gandhiji laid great stress on craft centred education. He said, "Literary education should follow the education of the hand, the one gift that visible distinguishes man from beast. It is a superstation to think that fullest development of man is impossible without a knowledge of the art of reading and writing. Knowledge undoubtedly adds grace to life, but it is no way indispensable for man's moral, physical or material growth. Manual work will have to be the centre of the whole thing. But manual training will not consist in producing articles for a school museum or toys which have no value. It should produce marketable articles. The children will not do this as children used to do under the whip in the early days of the factories. They will do it because it entertains them and stimulates their intellect." So emphasis on craft is considered as most important both from economic and instructional points of view.

Choosing of Crafts

According to Gandhiji's conception manual work or craft is the core or summum-bonum of basic education. It is pivot round which the whole curriculum is to revolve. It is not simply an additional subject in the curriculum as some people think. For the selection of crafts, the points given ahead must be borne in mind.

1. Craft should Consider the Psychology of Children. While a craft is being selected, we should consider the likes and dislikes of the children. Any craft in which the children do not take interest should not be forced upon them. Care should be taken for the selection of a craft. Craft should be such as considers their interests and natures and is also related to their present life.

2. Craft should be Productive. Craft in order to be useful, must be purposeful and productive. In other words it should be purposive. Craft should not be taken as activity done for the sake of activity alone. Why is there an insistance on the word 'productive'? It is so because the young children take great interest in something which is concrete and productive. The money realised from the sale proceeds of such a craft will give immense pleasure to the children.

3. Craft should be Used for Education. The idea of teaching craft is not to make children craftsmen. Rather these are to be exploited for educational purposes. The child should know the why and wherefore of every process. He is not to learn it mechanically.

4. Craft should be Basic. A basic craft is that which should find natural points of correlation with important human activities and interests. It should be craft around which various subjects of the curriculum can be groped. So craft should be basic.

5. Craft should be Selected According to Environments of the Place. It should consider the geographical conditions and social background of the community in which the school is situated. This presupposes that the crafts selected for rural areas will differ from those selected for urban areas. This would be related to the life. This principle would be extended to states. Crafts will differ from state to state because of diversities.

Advantages

The following will be some of the advantages if it is wisely chosen and scientifically taught:

(a) **Psychologically,** it will satisfy the child's instincts of play, self assertion and curiosity. It would be learning through doing.

(b) **Socially,** it will make him a good sociable creature. It will teach team work and dignity of labour. It shall remove

the hateful gulf between the manual and intellectual work. A child will become a good and useful member of the society.

(c) **Educationally,** it will make the children as co-sharers and active participants in the process of education. The development of hand and head will go pari-passu. Education will be natural, effective and attractive.

(d) **Economically,** it will help the children to stand on their own legs. They will develop self-confidence and reliance in themselves.

(e) **Morally,** it will build up the morals of the children. Right skills and attitudes will help in improving their morals.

Defects of the English System of Education

The traditional system of education was outdated and old. It did not satisfy the aspirations of the people. It was a foreign plant unsuited to Indian needs. It was expensive and harmful. It only aimed at producing clerks. It gave only literary education which crushed originality and rendered the people unfit for a fastly changing society.

The following were the defects of this education :

1. It was Isolated from Life. The courses of study were neither related to the daily life of children nor to the life of the society in which they were born and were living. They failed to solve the most ordinary problems of life.

2. It Failed to Develop the Whole Personality of the Child. The traditional system of education was not well conceived. It was one sided and narrow. It simply developed the mental faculty of the child. Information giving was the only aim of this education. No opportunities were provided for the development of skills, attitudes and training of emotions. It did not develop 'Hand, head and heart' simultaneously.

3. Excessive Stress on Examinations. It was too much ridden by examinations. The promotion of the students and teachers depended to a great extent upon the result of the final examination. Naturally both of them focussed their attention on the annual examination throughout the year. Real knowledge was neither given nor it was desired by the students. They put more reliance on cheap books. The examination fear crushed the activity and initiative of the students and also killed the originality and spirit of research and experimentation of the teacher.

4. Too much Dominated by English Language. Since 1837 when Macaulay decided in favour of English as the vehicle of instructions in schools, it continued to dominate. It gave a death blow to the Indian languages, with the result that only few could benefit from it. Moreover the Indian students could not express themselves in a foreign language. It served as an impediment for the mental growth of the children.

5. Poor Methods of Teaching. The teacher exercised full control over the teaching learning process. He was a demagogue and imparted knowledge in a mechanical way to the class. The teacher was active whereas the pupils were nothing more than passive listeners. The students had no other alternative except to memorise the information given by the teacher or cram up the matter given in the text-books. This procedure did not leave any initiative with the students. This very much discouraged the mental growth, rather they slavishly follow the teacher.

6. Moral Education Totally Ignored. The system of education was anything but Indian. Cultural heritage was altogether ignored. The pupils were only Indian in blood, but in habits, diet, dress and manners, they were foreigners. The pupils according to Gandhiji, were rendered aliens in their own country. Even an English gentleman Mr. Rawlinson was critical of such an education. He remarked, "The greatest wrong inflicted on Indian education by our educational policy has been on the spiritual side. We have uprooted a system based upon the traditional code of Ethics of the East. We have divorced religion from education."

7. Lack of Contact. Owing to the large number of classes no personal contact could be maintained by the teacher with his pupils. Our ancient education had succeeded in maintaining cordial relations between the teacher and the taught. As a matter of fact this contact was very much cherished. But this human factor was ignored with the result that much of the present indiscipline amongst student community ascribed to this lack of contact on the part of the teacher. Moreover, teachers taught different subjects to one class. This factor also discourged individual attention to students. Very naturally, such a system did not develop well balanced personalities of the pupils.

8. No Emphasis on Co-curricular Activities. The curriculum was heavy and flexible. It gave no place to co-curricular activities. These days education without it would appear lifeless. Insistence was placed on the study of books alone.

Essential Features of Basic Education

Gandhiji's concept of Basic Education aimed at the all-round development of the child. He was not an idealist; rather he was a realist. The Basic Education movement if given a fair trial can bring about a great revolution not only in the educational structure but in the economic and social spheres as well. The distinctive features of Basic Education are the following:

1. Child Centred. In this system of education, the main emphasis is on the child and his needs are studied, understood and satisfied. In fact activity and interest are its pillars or core. Education becomes a purposeful activity if these two aspects are properly kept in view. Instructions do not remain insipid and lifeless, but becomes interesting and attractive. Genuine interest is created. Basic Education does not ignore the present needs of the pupils.

2. Greater Freedom for the Teacher and the Taught. In basic education discipline does not mean order and external restraint but an intelligent use of freedom.

3. Psychologically Sound. Basic Education is 'psychologically' most sound. The child is not passive in the teaching learning process, but is an active participant. It prepares the child socially as well. It provides organised craft and community activities. It generates a sense of responsibility and confidence through participation in activities.

4. Related to Life. Basic Education is an education of life, for life and through life. The teacher, in this scheme, can give a proper shape to the life of the child. Like Froebel's Kindergarten, Basic school is a society in miniature, where the child is given practical training in all those activities of life in which he will be engaged in his adult life.

5. Basic Education not a Class Education. The ultimate objective of Basic Education is to create a social order in which there is no un-natural division between 'haves' and 'have nots'.

6. Sociologically Sound. Basic Education teaches adjustment in society and also dignity of labour. It overcomes the barriers that exist between manual and intellectual work. If followed properly, it can succeed in establishing a new social order.

7. Community Centred. Basic Education keeps in view the needs of the society in which the children live. Due regard is given to the special environments of the children before selecting a basic craft. These crafts relate to the vocations of the people with whom the children are so closely associated. Thus the children are naturally interested in them. It becomes easier for the children to learn those crafts and education becomes meaningful. No extra burden is put on them. In this way Basic Education is community centred because not only the children's interests are kept in view but also those of community in which the children spend most of their time.

8. Formation of Character. Apart from being an educationist, Gandhiji was a moralist as well. He stressed on character building. Basic Education lays great stress on the development of morals and character. Any education which did not aim at character formation, would be according to him, anything but education. His insistence on the training of heart, head and hand denotes universal love, devotion to duty, manual work and mental poise. This is what exactly character is.

9. Basic System is National in Character. Being a national system, it cuts at the root of traditional system. It is not a product of foreigners but truly represents Indian ideals, culture and civilisation. Academic education was correlated with vocational training to make it functional and useful. It preserves ancient culture. It is intended for all rather than for few privileged ones. Rightly it is a national system of education and satisfies the aspirations of the people of the country.

10. It is Flexible. Unlike the traditional system of education, Basic Education is flexible. It caters to the larger interests of the children. The basic craft can be selected according to local needs and conditions. One particular craft is not imposed upon for the entire community or country.

11. Emphasis on Mother Tongue. Gandhiji stressed that proper education can only be imported through the mother-tongue. Foreign tongue as the medium of instruction makes us unfit for original work. It makes us crammers and imitators.

12. It is an all Round Scheme. It is a scheme for all the individuals. Though the main emphasis is on the elementary education, yet it covers all stages and links naturally all the stages so nicely together.

13. Ideal of Citizenship. Basic Education encourages cooperative activities and through these corporate life. It lays the foundations of ideal citizenship.

14. Correlation. Basic Education insists on correlated and integrated studies. It does not divide knowledge into water-tight compartments nor does it encourage book learning. Correlation of knowledge with three main centres is recommended *viz (i)* in the basic craft *(ii)* the social environment of the child, *(iii)* the physical environment. In this way learning is correlated with the actual life of the child. Learning becomes purposive.

❐

6

Education in Public Schools

The public school system was transplanted in India by the British administrators for the benefit of their own children. The first Public School, the Bishop Cotton School at Simla was established in 1856.

Then many Public Schools like Lawrence School, Lovedale; Lawrence School, Sanawar; Scindia School, Gwalior; Daly College, Indore; Mayo College, Ajmer; Prince of Wales Military College, Dehradun (under the Ministry of Defence); Raj Kumar College, Raipur; Raj Kumar College, Rajkot; Sandul Public School, Bikaner; Sardar's School, Gwalior; Shivaji Military School, Poona; Doon School Dehradun; Modern School, New Delhi; Maharani Gayatri Devi Girls School, Jaipur; Yadvendra Public School, Patiala were started.

The number of the Member Schools of the Indian Public Schools Conference as on 10th December 1969 was 44.

It should be noted that the public schools in India are of recent origin. A few of them have grown out of Chief's Colleges but the majority among them are the products of the post-independence period. Both in the time of their origin and in the purpose for which they were established they differ widely. The differences among them also lie in number of seats available, facilities for games and sports, fees and numerous other details of administration and financial support.

Even so they have a few common features *e.g.*, they are all secondary institutions (though some of them continue to be called colleges), they are mostly residential, hence their students prepared for the India School Certificate Examination and their headmasters are members of Indian Public School Conference.

Contribution of King Canute (1180 A.D.). The first English "Public School" came into existence in the year 1180 A. D. during the reign of King Canute who is remembered as having been so great a lover of religion that he established Public Schools in the cities and towns, appointing masters to them, and sending to them to be taught well-born boys of good promise, and meeting the expenses from the royal purse.

Winchester and Eton School. Winchester School was started in 1387 A.D. by William of Wykeham, Bishop Winchester. The good features of the school were a close link between a college and the university, residential facilities, students drawn from all parts of the country, the charitable intention to aid poor scholars and to provide recruits for the service of the Church.

In 1440, the foundation of Eton School was laid by King Henry VI, following the model at Winchester. Both of these institutions were founded with the intention of promoting the cause of religion.

Other Public Schools. Many more public schools like Shrewsburry (1571), Rugby (1567), Harrow (1571), Chatter-house (1611) were started and still they are well known all over the world for their high standard of education. Some of the characteristics of these schools are superior teaching staff, superior courses of teaching, superior library, residential character, perfect system, house system and high discipline. Our late Prime Minister, Pandit Jawahar Lal Nehru received his early education at Harrow Public School.

TYPES OF PUBLIC SCHOOLS

All the public schools in India can be placed in the following categories:

1. Schools for Indian Princely Families. Mayo College, Ajmer; Raj Kumar College, Rajpur; Raj Kumar College, Rajkot etc. come under this category.

2. Schools for Europeans and Anglo-Indians. Bishop Cotton School, Simla; Lawrence School, Sanawar (Simla Hills); Lawrence School, Lovedale (Nigiris) were of this kind and they were mostly meant for foreigners and Anglo-Indians. Now these schools are open to Indians.

3. Sainik and Military Schools. These schools have been started on the lines of King George's Schools and Lawrence Schools. The aim of these schools is to impart training for leadership for the Indian Army. Some of the Sainik Schools are: Sainik School, Kapurthala (Punjab); Sainik School, Kunjpura (Karnal); Sainik School, Bijapur (Mysore); Sainik School, Chittorgarh (Rajasthan); Sainik School, Jamnagar (Gujarat); Sainik School, Rewa (Madhya Pradesh); Sainik School, Satara (Maharashtra); Sainik School, Purulia (West Bengal); Sainik School, Bhubaneshwar (Orissa); Sainik School, (Amravathi-Nagar (Madras); Sainik School, P. O. Sarojini Nagar (Lucknow); Shri Shivaji Preparatory Military School, Poona; Dholpur Military School, Dholpur; Military School, Bangalore; Belgaum Military School, Belgaum; Chail Military School, Chail (Simla Hills).

4. Ordinary Public Schools. Like Doon School, Dehradun; Modern School, New Delhi; Delhi Public School, Delhi; Punjab Public School, Nabha; Birla Public School, Pilani (Rajasthan); Birla Vidya Mandir, Nainital (U.P.).

Special Features of Public Schools

1. Residential. Public schools are generally residential in nature. Students and teachers stay on the same campus and live like members of the same family. The child soon becomes a responsible, self-reliant and independent individual. It is not the mother who mothers his needs every time.

2. Character Building and Leadership Training. Public schools emphasise character building, moral training, discipline and training in leadership. They develop resourceful-ness, originality, fellow-feeling and organisational abilities. They are trained to be honest, courageous, tolerent, alert and well disciplined.

3. Control. Public schools are generally controlled by an elected body of the people. They are financed by the people. The 'Department of Public Instructions' has nothing to do with it, like inspection etc. Public schools are independent in following their own courses of study, time-table, methods of teaching and co-curricular activities etc.

4. Financially Stable. Public schools are financially stable. They agree to send annually a copy of its audited sheet and statement of accounts to the Honorary Secretary of the Conference.

5. Adequate Buildings and Equipment. Public schools have adequate buildings and spacious accommoda-tion. They have beautiful and well developed lawns and playing fields. They are well equipped according to physical and mental levels of their pupils. They provide equipment for out-of-school activities other than games.

6. Qualified and Well Paid Staff. They keep highly qualified and well paid staff. They enjoy social status and security. The conditions of service of staff members are highly congenial. They are given a number of facilities like residential accomodation, free medical aid, free education of their children and meals at low cost.

7. Extensive Education. In public schools, extensive education is provided. The general academic and social environment of public schools is rich. The child is kept busy from morning till evening.

These schools have extensive programmes of various co-curricular activities like debates, declamations, poetic recitation, writing articles, games and sports, dancing, music, swimming, painting etc. Students choose various activities according to their interests and aptitudes. Sports and games are compulsory for all.

8. Medium of Instruction. Generally, public schools have English as the medium of instruction. But Hindi, the national language of India is not ignored. There is stress on conversation and in building vocabulary.

9. Standard of Examination. Public schools prepare students for a public examination of the standard of the Cambridge School Certificate and provide facilities for education beyond this stage.

10. Course of Study. Public schools provide a course of study extending over atleast five academic years beyond the age 11.

11. Admissions. Admission is open to all without any consideration of caste or creed. Admissions are made on the basis of test and interview. Admission to Sainik Schools is vigorous.

12. Prefect System. In public schools prefects are entrusted with various responsibilities and share the task of maintaining proper discipline. Thus they economise the work of the staff.

13. House System. House is one of the special features of the organisation of public schools. House is the administrative unit which provides a family atmosphere and builds healthy spirit of emulation. Individual attention is paid to each and every child for the harmonious development of his personality.

14. Medical Inspection and Remedial Treatment. Public schools provide for adequate medical inspection and remedial treatment.

Some Views Concerning Importance of Public Schools

Views of Dr. K. L. Shrimali. Emphasising the features and importance of public schools Dr. K. L. Shrimali at the 20th Annual Meeting of the Indian Public Schools Headmasters' Conference remarked, "No body denies that public schools in this country provide good education. Boys who come out of these schools have poise and self confidence, qualities which are greatly needed in our public life. These schools provide facilities for physical education and games, character training and intellectual development, which we would like to introduce in ordinary schools also. In matters of educational standards too, these schools have little to be desired and we would like all our schools to strive to attain the same standard."

View of Dr. Zakir Hussain. In February 1968, while speaking at the Thirteenth Session of the Indian Public Schools Conference held at the Modern School, New Delhi, Dr. Zakir Hussain observed, "I would like the institutions which belong to this conference to be distinct by three important features, namely:

(i) All India character and significant contribution to national integration.

(ii) Progressive outlook and leadership in educational experimentation; and

(iii) Maintenance of good standards."

View of Secondary Education Commission. "There are greater opportunities in these (public) schools than in the majority of secondary schools for developing certain essential traits of character, including the qualities of leadership, because of the special facilities that they can offer and the close contact between teachers and pupils that is possible in them."

View of Kort Hahn. "They (public schools) instill fairness in anger, coolness in danger, grace in defeat, readiness for service at all times how to argue without quarrelling, how to quarrel without suspecting, how to suspect without slandering."

View of Sir John Sargent. Sir John Sargent, formerly Educational Adviser to the Government of India remarked, "The product of the public school displays a capacity to set up, and abide by, standards of conduct and readiness to accept responsibility, qualities which must form an essential part of the equipment of any real public servant."

View of Principal H. L. Dutt. In an article in *Hindustan Times* dated 21st May, 1972, Principal H. L. Dutt of the Colvin Taluqdar's College pointed out the following features of the public schools: "The public school boy, I hope, does his best in the walk of life he enters. The contribution (of public schools) in all fields is significant. Their products are scientists, doctors, teachers, artists, social workers, members of legislatures, ministers and what have you... Because of better atmosphere in a public school a teacher finds it more conducive to his calling, and takes more interest in his work."

Future of Public Schools in India

In spite of the criticism levied against public schools valid place in the future reconstruction of education in our country. They have to stay on account of the following reasons:

1. Right to Exist in Democratic Countries. Public schools have every right to exist in the democratic countries on the following grounds:

(i) Right of the Parents to Choose the Kind of Education. According to Article 26(3) of the Constitution,

"Parents have a prior right to choose the kind of education that should be given to their child." It is the right of the parents to decide whether they are to send their children to public school, government school or other type of school. If public schools are closed then it will be the negation of democratic principle.

(ii) ***Right to Open Institutions.*** According to Article 30 of Indian Constitution "All minorities whether based on religion or language shall have the right to establish and administer educational institutions of their choice." Thus all communities and religious sects have the freedom of opening their own institutions. Public schools have been criticised on the ground that they are Anglo-Indian in character. It should be pointed out that Anglo-Indian Community in our country is as patriotic as any other community. Moreover public schools are run not by one particular community but by many social groups and educational societies.

(iii) ***Right of Equal Opportunity.*** Democratic society believes in the equality of rights and opportunities for all. It means that education should be provided to all children for their full growth and all round development according to their capacities, capabilities and natural endowment. It should be kept in mind that democracy does not believe in providing identical opportunities. Identical opportunities improve the same type of education for all children irrespective of their abilities, aptitudes and other endowments. Kothari Commission's idea of providing identical education to all under Common School System is undemocratic.

2. Controversy not Based on Educational Principles. The controversy over the public school is not basd on educational principles but on social and economic problems. Public schools are criticised on the ground that monetary sacrifices are needed. In fact monetary sacrifices are needed for getting the best facilities in every field. Even the medical facilities of the highest order cost too much and therefore are not within the reach of many people. Everybody cannot afford to purchase the best means of transport *e.g.* a car, to purchase a first class railway ticket or of air-conditioned bus, to dine in a first cass hotel and similarly to get the best educational facilities. The proper approach lies not in banning the best facilities but in raising the standard of living of the people. Socialistic pattern of society does not aim at distribution of poverty but on the contrary it aims at the conversion of poverty into prosperity.

3. Justification for High Fees. The fees charged by the public school are justified on the grounds that the schools receive no grants from the State nor would they like to receive any grant if conditions are imposed because that would deprive them of their independence to recruit the best type of staff and the best type of children, and to spend generously on equipping the various departments within the school without being subjected to long procedure delays.

4. Institutions of Quality. Public schools are institutions of quality. These schools provide the best qualified staff, proper equipment, appropriate pupil-teacher ratio and ideal conditions. Democracy neither prevents the manufacture of quality good nor it stands in the way of training quality students. A common school is not expected to do full justice on qualitative side. From this point of view we refute the argument that public schools are not needed in the present Socialistic Pattern of Society.

5. Public Schools are not Meant for Rich Pupils Alone. The argument that all the public schools should be abolished because they produce a type of person who is arrogant and that they cater only to the rich, can be advanced only by an ignorant person. The Government of India selects brilliant children of low income group parents every year on the basis of competitive examinations and sends them to selected public schools at its own expenses. Thus public schools provide education to both rich and poor students alike.

Suggestions Concerning Future of Public Schools in India

The following suggestions can be of much use concerning the future of Public School System in India.

1. Criterion of Admission. The admission to public schools must strictly be on a free and equal basis whether it is by application or by competitive tests.

2. Representative of Central Government. The Governing Body of the school may have one representative of the Central Government.

3. Competent Indian Staff. In the public schools we should have competent Indian staff—Indian in mind, body and spirit and not incompetent, ill-qualified Europeans and missionaries. The staff should have enthusiastic and experimental outlook. The staff should be recruited on a strictly all-India basis.

4. Indian Outlook. The educational life of the public schools should be in conformity with Indian culture, traditions and national outlook.

5. Constitution of the School. The Constitution of the public school should be in conformity with the overall educational aims of such schools.

6. Drastic Reforms in Curricula. Drastic reforms should be made in the curricula of public schools. More stress should be laid on subjects like Science and Mathematics. We should not be very rigid on the medium of instruction in public schools. Undue emphasis on English should not be laid and due attention should be paid to the study of Indian languages.

7. Dissolution of Unhealthy Differences. There should be no unhealthy distinction between the public schools and the common schools. Unhealthy differences should be checked. Public schools should be common schools in the sense that they should cater to the needs of the gifted children without any distinction of economic status. Provision should be made for gifted students of ordinary schools for joining the public schools.

8. Increasing the Number of Sainik Schools. The number of Sainik schools should be increased, as they cater to the defence needs of the country.

9. Conversion into Experimental Schools. Public schools should be converted into experimental schools and the research work done in the public schools should be carefully studied and its useful results should be carried out in other schools.

❒

7

Higher Education

Higher education in India has a long historical past. Universities like Nalanda (located in Bihar) were well known all over the world. The Chinese pilgrims visiting India between 400 BC and AD 800 referred in their travel accounts to the excellent work being done by these universities. The existence of flourishing institutions of higher learning in ancient India is also attested by significant developments in intellectual fields like literature, literary criticism, philosophy logic, medicine, mathematics and astronomy. Universities as institutions appear to have declined in the Middle Ages but the pursuit of higher learning was continued by individual scholars. After the advent of the British in the 19th Century, higher education in India was put in a westernised mould with English as the medium of instruction and with the introduction of new subjects. The first three universities in the modern sense were established in the three metropolitan towns of Calcutta, Bombay and Madras in 1857. A conscious attempt to regulate governance of higher education was made with the University Act 1904. By 1947, at independence, there were 16 universities in India.

Characteristics of Higher Education in India

The characteristics of the higher education system in India are dominated by the educational system of which higher education is a part; the expansion in various dimensions of higher education and institutional diversity.

Scale. As a result of the system of education developed during the last 150 years, India has now more than 120 universities or similar institutions and 4500 affiliated colleges. This has given India one of the largest trained high-level manpower bases in the world. This is not surprising in the second most populous country in the world.

Expansion. The expansion of higher education since independence has been phenomenal. The student enrolment increased from 0.23 million in 1947-48 to 2.65 million in 1979-80. The number of institutions increased from 16 universities in 1947-48 to 108 universities, 11 institutions deemed to be universities and 9 institutions of national importance in 1979-80. In 1976-77 there were 166,742 teachers in the universities. The total enrolment in collegiate general education courses in 1976-77 was 5.1 per cent of the population in the corresponding age-group 18-23, of which the proportion of boys was, 7.3 per cent and the proportion of girls was 2.8 per cent. The plan and non-plan budgeted expenditure on higher education in 1980-81 in the country as a whole was 3750 million; 13 per cent of the total expenditure on education.

Institutional Diversity. India has a federal polity with states as constituent units. The subject of education, including higher education, is a concurrent one. In other words, both the state governments and central government can legislate in the field. Normally, the establishment of universities in India is under state legislation. However, there are also a few universities which are established under a central enactment. Then there are central bodies which are concerned with general problems of coordination and maintenance of standards or of promotion of research in an all-India perspective. Against this background, the institutions in the field of higher education are categorized as follows:

1. There are about 85 state universities of the teaching and the affiliating type which cover not only arts, science, and commerce subjects but also medicine and engineering.
2. After 1965, agricultural universities were established in various states concerned not only with imparting agricultural instruction but also with research and extension of research results to the field. There are 20 such universities.
3. Central universities were established in response to specific historical situations. Banaras, Aligarh and Delhi Universities were established prior to independence. Visva-Bharati was established to fulfil the educational objectives of the Poet Rabindra Nath Tagore, and Jawaharlal Nehru University was established to fulfil objectives like democracy, socialism and international understanding dear to Jawaharlal Nehru. Northeastern Hill University caters to three states in northeast region and Hyderabad University is a central university in the southern part of the country. There is also the interstate University of Punjab at Chandigarh.
4. There are also four institutes of Management which, though not set up by an act of Parliament, are also all-India institutions promoted by central government according to a pre-determined pattern.
5. There are nine institutions of national importance established by an act of Parliament. These include the All-India Institute of Medical Sciences, Delhi, Post-graduate Institute for Medical Research and Education at Chandigarh, and the Indian Institutes of Technology.
6. Some educational institutions have distinguished themselves in selected fields like rural reconstruction,

social work and integrated education, though they are not universities in the traditional sense. These are institutions deemed to be universities. A leading example of the category is Jamia Millia Islamia in Delhi, established by the late Dr. Zakir Hussain who apart from being the President of India was also a distinguished educationist in the field of basic education. The Indian Institute of Science, Bangalore is also deemed a university. There are 12 such institutions.

There are four categories of apex institutions set up for specific purposes relating to higher education.

(a) The University Grants Commission (UGC) established in 1956 coordinates and determines standards in the universities and for that purpose makes maintenance, development and specified grants available to various institutions. All the universities and deemed universities and the colleges function under the umbrella of the UGC.

(b) The National Institute of Educational Planning and Administration undertakes research in educational planning and administration, provides training and consultancy services in the field and arranges orientation for senior administrators from the central government and states and collaborates with other countries, especially in the Asian region.

(c) As it was seen that the traditional department-faculty university framework was not conducive to the promotion and development of research in priority disciplines the government established national councils devoted to the promotion of research in specific disciplines. The Indian Council of Social Science Research was established in 1969 the Indian Council of Historical Research was established in

1972, the Indian Council of Philosophy was established in 1977 and reactivated in 1987.

(d) The Indian Institute of Advanced Study at Shimla established in 1965 provides an environment suitable for academic research and undertakes, organises guides and promotes advanced research in selected subjects in the humanities, Indian culture, comparative religion, social sciences and natural sciences.

New Developments in the 1980

To deal with the expansion and to problems of higher education, the Sixth Five-Year Plan (1980-85) aimed to:

(i) promote the values of secularism, democracy, national integration and dignity of labour throughout the educational system;

(ii) improve higher education courses so as to increase the component of learning from real life situations through participation in socially relevant activities;

(iii) consolidate existing facilities for higher education and programmes with minimum additional inputs for quality improvement and physical infrastructure and coordinate higher education with opportunities for employment, especially self-employment and developmental goals;

(iv) sensitise academic communities to the problems of poverty, illiteracy and environmental degradation through organised participation in poverty reduction and environment improvement programmes.

(v) promote selective growth in educational fields of national importance and social relevance such as the pursuit of scholarship and excellence in basic sciences and humanities, development of scientific and technical manpower, human resource development among weaker sections, socially handicapped groups and women, and to provide essential commodities needed by students at controlled prices.

Guidelines

The UGC is to tailor its assistance to the requirements of the objectives of removal of regional disparities in higher education facilities and also to improve the standards and quality of education. Non-viable colleges will be assisted to become viable over a period of years. Assistance to colleges in backward districts and in tribal areas will be in accordance with relaxed norms. State governments and universities will be encouraged to lay down criteria for opening new colleges so that non-viable colleges are not brought into existence in future.

So far as universities are concerned, the main emphasis is to be on improvement of standards and making extension an integral part of the activities of the institutions of higher education. Expansion of educational facilities both by way of opening new universities and university centres for postgraduate studies or new departments, has low priority. An optimum balance between undergraduate and postgraduate stage of education will be maintained.

Universities which have reached a critical size and development will be asked to restrict enrolment in formal and full-time instructional programmes. Demands for increase in enrolment will be met through correspondence courses, extended and evening classes, by increasing enrolment in colleges and by allowing students to appear as private students. About 17 universities in India are already offering correspondence courses. Mysore university also follows an 'open' admission policy for its correspondence courses.

Structure, Number and Types of Institutions

There are following types of institutions of higher education in India:

1. Central universities established by Acts of Central Legislature which are at present seven in number.
2. Thirteen institutions notified as deemed universities by Central Government by virtue of their contribution to innovation in higher education in India.
3. State universities established by Acts of State or Provincial Legislatures. At present these are 111 in number of which 21 are Agricultural Universities.
4. Nine institutions of national importance established by an Act of Parliament, which can award degrees, namely, All India Institute of Medical Sciences, Delhi; Postgraduate Institute of Medical Education and Research, Chandigarh; Indian Institutes of Technology, at Bombay, Delhi, Madras, Kanpur and Kharagpur; Indian Statistical Institute, Calcutta and Dakshin Bharat Hindi Prachar Sabha, Madras; three National Institutes of Management located respectively at Ahmedabad, Calcutta and Bangalore.

Thus the total institutions of higher learning in India are 143. About 4886 colleges referred above normally work under the umbrella of either a central university or a state university and are not able to award degrees independently. The Acts of the universities normally provide for various officers and authorities for the management of the universities. The head of the state is the nominal head of the university and is called the Visitor in the case of central universities and Chancellor in the case of state universities. The Vice-Chancellor is the academic and administrative head of a university and is normally appointed by the central government or the state government from out of a panel of names recommended by a selection committee. Eminent academics or administrators are normally appointed as Vice-Chancellors. They work through the Executive Council (Syndicate) and are also subject to overall supervision of a deliberative body which is variously called either court or senate. In curricular matters, Vice-Chancellors are advised by Academic Councils which are predominantly composed of academics. Subject to budgetary and financial constraints, universities are structurally designed to be autonomous in their functioning.

Students Enrolment. The student enrolment has gone up from 2,00,000 in 1947 to 29,52,066 in 1981-82. The average growth rate of enrolment during the decade 1972-73 to 1981-82 was 3.7 per cent per annum as against 12.1 per cent during 1962-63 to 1971-72. During the five year period from 1977-78 to 1981-82, the average annual compound growth rate of enrolment was 3.6 per cent. These rates vary from state to state, some states registering negative growth rate while other states registering three time the average growth rate. These variations were partly due to adjustments in adopting 10+2+3 pattern of education.

In the overall enrolment of 29,52,066, women accounted for 8,16,704 representing 27.7 per cent of enrolment. Since independence, the enrolment of women has gone up by approximately 20 times while the proportion of women to men has increased three-fold during the same period. This growth is accounted for only partly by the increase in the number of women colleges which stood at 624 in 1981-82.

In the post-independence period, there was also emphasis on enhancement in the educational opportunities for the weaker sections of the society and, in particular, scheduled castes and scheduled tribes which enjoy constitutional protection. This was done through reservation of seats and was also a part of the general expansion of higher education due to upward push exerted by out-turns of secondary education system. In 1977-78, out of the total undergraduate enrolment of 22,55,306, scheduled castes numbered 1,69,662 or 7.5 per cent and scheduled tribes numbered 35,495 or 16 per cent. In the same year, out of total postgraduate enrolment of 2,33,644, scheduled castes numbered 17,592 or 7.5 per cent and scheduled tribes numbered 2990 or 1.3 per cent.

About 40.3 percent students were enrolled in Arts Faculty, 21.3 per cent in Commerce Faculty, and 19.6 per cent in Science Faculty. Affiliated colleges accounted for 83.2 per cent of the total enrolment.

Teachers. In 1981-82, there were 42,186 teachers in the, University departments and university colleges. Out of them, 4170 were Professors, 9299 were Readers, 26,648 were Lecturers and 2069 were Tutors and Demonstrators. The staff in the affiliated colleges totalled 1,57,718 teachers in 1981-82 including 15,599 senior teachers, 1,34,019 Lecturers and 8100 Tutors and Demonstrators. The number of teaching staff has gone up from 37,142 in 1977-78 to 42,186 in 1981-82. The staff in the affiliated colleges has gone up from 1,41,202 in 1977-78 to 1,57,718 in 1981-82.

Administration. In day-to-day administration, the Vice-Chancellor is assisted by the registry finance office and examination branch. These are headed by senior administrative officers called Registrar, Finance Officer and Controller of Examination respectively. Registrar and Controller of Examinations tend to be internally recruited. The heads of finance branches however are normally recruited from organized Accounts and Audit Services of the state/central government. The Registrar is assisted by Deputy Registrars and Assistant Registrars, Ministerial staff and menial staff. This fourfold hierarchy of staffing is also found in other branches.

Source of Financing. The government provides the major funding of almost all institutions of higher learning. The funding is of two types—funding for maintenance and funding for development. In the case of central universities, maintenance funding is by the central government and in the case of state universities, it is by the state government. In the case of development, the major funding is through the University Grants Commission established in 1956 for the coordination and determination of standards in the country as a whole. The University Grants Commission makes institutional development grants as well as grants for quality improvement programmes to central universities and state universities. Some of the grants, especially, the building grants are given on a sharing basis. University Grants Commission also makes financial assistance for development available to viable affiliated colleges of the universities. The development assistance is given within the framework of the Five Year Plans.

The other sources of income are fees and endowments. During the recent years, the fees as a source of income have dwindled from 10 per cent to 5 per cent in most of the universities. Endowment as a source of income is almost negligible with the erosion in the value of income accruing from fixed endowments made several years back.

So far as colleges are concerned, they receive grant-in-aid from the respective state governments according to Grant-in-Aid Codes which lay down items of approved expenditure, the rest of the expenditure being required to be met by the management of the respective colleges which in some cases could be government owned and managed but in a large number of cases are under private management.

Policy Concerning Higher Education

National Policy Relating to Roles of Institutions of Higher Learning. Institutions of higher learning are multi-functional. They are expected to perform a series of roles like teaching, research, out-turn of education manpower for the developmental tasks of nation-building in various fields including management, research and development and finally a general up-gradation of the quality of the working population of the country. Institutions of higher learning, specially universities are also expected to get actively involved in the development tasks through the following:

(i) Participation in Adult Education and Continuing Education programme;

(ii) Provision of individual or institutional consultancy for policy making and expert roles; and

(iii) Actual involvement in development of community by adoption of villages or by adoption of selected programmes of plan development like Eco-Development, Regional Development, Industrial Development, etc.

Direction of Future Development

Since 1971, central government has followed a policy of discouraging the proliferation of institutions of higher learning *viz* both universities and colleges. Guidelines have been laid down for new universities to be eligible for financial assistance which contemplate that they should come into existence after a broad academic survey and only to fulfil a felt-need or to promote regional development. Indiscriminate growth of colleges is also to be discouraged. Non-viable colleges, that is, colleges with less than prescribed enrolment and staffing are not eligible for development assistance.

It is recognised that considering the expansion of secondary education, the enrolment in higher education is bound to increase. However, the endeavour is to provide for vocationalisation of lower courses so that only the students with correct motivation enter the higher educational stream. The three-year degree course is also being restructured so as to incorporate elements of job-orientation in the course so that graduates are able to find a job after completion of their degree.

Another important aim of the development of higher education is to provide non-formal avenues of education. This is being done through correspondence courses. At present 22 universities run approved correspondence courses. There has been apparent stagnation in the enrolment in correspondence courses because of a preconception about standards. The University Grants Commission is appraising the correspondence courses with a view to improve their quality and to make them more attractive. As a complementary measure, some states have started an Open University system on the UK model.

It is also proposed to give emphasis on important aspects of what may be called "development education" in the curricula. This comprises population education, environmental education, national integration education, and similar components of enrichment education.

It is also proposed to strengthen the research capabilities of the higher education system and to integrate their functioning with the research and development establishments in the government sector, namely, national laboratories.

University Autonomy. As indicated earlier, university legislation is designed to ensure the functioning of the universities as autonomous organisations under the supervision of the Chancellor Nisitor and subject to the budgetary constraints. The autonomy elements in the field of curriculum have broadly remained unaffected till recently. However, the academic autonomy is subject to the guidelines laid down by the University Grants Commission. There are also trends towards closer supervision of the university functioning in the financial and administrative matters by the Parliamentary Committees. This can be said to be part of a universal phenomenon. Lastly, the power of the purse exercised by the state/central government modifies the autonomy of the universities in matters relating to staffing levels and terms and conditions of service and remuneration.

Relationship Among Different Types of Post-secondary Institutions. As indicated above, there are two main types of institutions, namely, colleges and universities which are in a hierarchical relationship. However, some of the colleges by dint of their historical standing and academic standards do enjoy a leadership position *vis-a-vis* their university. There are also certain gradations between different universities apart from the natural distinction between state universities and central universities. All the universities function under the developmental umbrella of the University Grants Commission and look up to it for a leadership role.

In relation to research funding in specific fields like social sciences, historical sciences and philosophy, apex bodies like Indian Council of Social Science Research, Indian Council of Historical Research and Indian Council of Philosophical Research have come up which have taken over part of the funding of research in these respective fields. This funding is normally on the basis of fellowships or projects.

Most of the statutes of the universities provide for collaboration between sister institutions. Such a collaboration naturally takes place among central universities and also among universities located in a particular state. The committee of vice-chancellors of central universities under the chairmanship of chairman, University Grants Commission and the committee of vice-chancellors at state universities under the chairmanship of respective chancellors play a coordinating role. The coloration among institutions, however, takes place across the centre/state divide and also across state boundaries according to disciplinary interests of the faculty.

Student Admission. Different universities follow their own criteria of eligibility of students for admission to their institutions. This basically provides for getting a minimum percentage of marks at the higher secondary level (35 to 40 per cent). Technical and professional institutions conduct their own entrance tests prior to entry. The admissions are related to the capacities in terms of staff, laboratory and library facilities. In colleges and certain popular subjects, however, the capacity ceilings tend to be pierced. It is only in the technical and professional colleges and in certain science subjects that admission ceilings are strictly adhered to.

Migration of students from one university to another depends on recognition of equivalence by the respective universities. Universities are autonomous in this regard though certain broad guidelines are laid down by the Association of Indian Universities. There is no central mechanism for coordination of admissions except in the case of technical and professional fields.

Higher Education and Manpower Planning

Although the out-turn of higher education feeds into the job market, the projections of manpower are restricted to professional technical-education. Till 1960s, there was continuous expansion in technical streams which, however, was curbed following perceptible unemployment among the engineering graduates. Recently, the policy has been reviewed and some expansion in the technical and professional courses has been permitted.

One aspect of manpower planning is the types of courses which are offered and become popular. Of late, the popularity of commerce courses in preference to arts courses indicates the greater employment potential of the commerce education as against liberal arts education. There has, however, been no perceptible diminution in the number going in for arts courses because sections earlier deprived of educational opportunities like women, weaker sections, etc, prefer to go in for arts courses in the initial stages.

The Institute of Applied Manpower Research at New Delhi has conducted some research studies relating to demand and supply for technical manpower in India. However, predictive models feeding into the policy-making have not been developed so far. An effort in this direction has recently been initiated by the Technical Education Wing of the Ministry of Education.

Equitable Distribution of Educational Opportunities

The equity in educational opportunities has several dimensions, namely, regional, community and sex. These are dealt with as follows:

Traditionally, the hinterlands of major metropolises like Calcutta, Chennai and Mumbai have accounted for bulk of enrolment in higher education. After independence, these disparities in regional distribution have tended to be reduced. There has been increase in the number of institutions, both universities and colleges in northern states which also happen to be more populous. It cannot, however, be said that differences in the educational development as measured in terms of out-turn of graduates as between states, can be eliminated in the near future.

So far as weaker communities and women are conceded, reference has been made earlier to the expansion in educational opportunities for these sections. As indicated, scheduled castes and scheduled tribes accounted for 7.5 per cent of enrolment in 1977-78 and scheduled tribes accounted for 1.6 per cent enrolment in the same year. This enrolment though impressive was much less than the share of these communities in the population (15 per cent and ½ per cent). Similarly, there has been an increase in the enrolment of women from 22.7 percent in 1971-72 to 27.7 per cent in 1981-82. This, however, is much less than the sex distribution of the population which is roughly equal.

Special measures have been taken to increase the enrolment of educationally deprived sections by provision of incentives in the form of scholarships, etc. Some states are classified as educationally backward and as such are eligible for higher financial assistance from the central government.

Planning and Programmes of Higher Education

National/State Level Planning. In socio-economic development, India has adopted the method of medium-term planning extending over five years. There is a Planning Commission at the national level which coordinates the process of formulation and implementation in all sectors, of programmes at all levels including state and sub-state levels. The ministries/departments at the national and state levels are an integral part of this planning process. At the national level, for example, Ministry of Education is allocated an outlay for the educational sector as a whole excluding medical and agricultural education. This outlay is subdivided into school education, higher education, technical education and other components of the educational programme according to priorities. As indicated earlier, at present universalization of primary education is a priority of educational policy and hence is entitled to a lion's share of funding. The outlay of educational sector also includes a summation of all outlays of the various state governments which depends on several factors including resource mobilization and priorities of the state governments as adjusted within national priorities. So far as medical education and agricultural education are concerned, a similar exercise is performed by Health Ministry and Agriculture Ministry respectively.

Institutions Involved and Process of Planning at Institutional Level. It will be seen that the institutions involved in the planning process comprise Planning Commission, Education Ministry and University Grants Commission at the national level and the Education

Departments of the state governments at the regional level. The universities are brought into the process of planning through the mechanism of visiting teams sent by University Grants Commission in connection with every Five Year Plan Period. The visiting teams are normally sent at the inception of the plan period and make an assessment of academic and administrative requirements of the university in the next five years keeping in view the stage of development reached, the priorities of policy and financial constraints. University Grants Commission on the basis of the recommendations of the visiting teams, decides on ceilings for institutional development for a particular institution.

Mechanism for Institutional Planning. The institutional planning and review take place through the statutory bodies like Academic Council, Finance Committee and the Executive Council. The Vice-chancellor, in consultation with various faculties, prepares his proposals for the five year plan and submits the same to the visiting committee. The report of the Visiting Committee is drafted after close consultation with the Vice-chancellor and the faculty. Naturally, all the projected requirements of a university may not be met within the ceiling recommended by visiting committee and accepted by the University Grants Commission.

The review and monitoring system is built into the process of planning. While there are quarterly reviews in respect of most of the programmes, an annual review, in any case, takes place in connection with the formulation of an annual plan which is part of the annual budget. It is at this stage that various changes and developments are taken into account to make corrective adjustments.

Apart from the review of the academic programme of the university which is taken up by the visiting committees appointed by the University Grants Commission, several institutions have statutory provisions for a five-yearly or seven-yearly review of their functioning for chalking out future lines of development. In addition, by virtue of visitorial/Chancellor supervision, universities are also subject to visitorial enquiry/inspecting which could take place at any time. The policy of the government, however, has been to go in for visitorial enquiries only in extreme circumstances and as far as possible, rely on normal academic planning and administrative reviews whose results are to be fed into the policy formulation.

Major National/State Development Programmes for Higher Education. The National Development Programmes for Higher Education are formulated and implemented mainly by the University Grants Commission. The University Grants Commission gives assistance to institutions for the following purposes:

(i) institutional development;

(ii) faculty improvement programmes which include assistance for organisation of seminars, symposia, workshops, institutes, etc, awards of national associates, national lecturers, teacher fellowships, travel grants, visiting professors, fellows, utilisation of services of retired teachers and career awards;

(iii) support for research through fellowships, through major research projects, through assistance to selected departments which are of two levels, namely, *(a)* centres of advanced study, *(b)* departments of special assistance;

(iv) assistance for adult and continuing education and for correspondence courses.

This assistance is over and above the development assistance that would be flowing to state level institutions through the respective state governments. The programmes of the state governments include, apart from establishment of new institutions, new academic schemes to supplement those devised by UGC in the particular context of the States requirements.

Institutional Management

Quality and Capacity of Academic Administration. The academic administration is headed by the vice-chancellor who is normally an eminent academic specialising in some discipline. He would normally be selected because of proven qualities of administrative leadership, initiative and experience. Earlier there was a tendency of drawing people from professions like judges, civil service, diplomats, etc, to head institutions. This tendency has been reversed and it is only in exceptional cases that non-academics are appointed to head the institutions.

The capacity of academic administration would depend on the administrative staff support available to the Vice-chancellor, cooperation extended by academic colleagues and the external environment of the university. Of late, the factors operating in external environment including extra academic factors and the pressures of individual constituents of the university community, namely, teachers, non-teaching employees and students have exerted major influence on the functioning of institutions. Adverse environmental factors have several times involved institutions into disturbances and closures. Assistance of "law and order" authorities is also required to be sought.

Efficiency of Institutions of Higher Education. It is difficult to measure the efficiency of an institution of higher education in the absence of unique and agreed criteria. Noting that universities are multi-functional institutions, their efficiency could be measured in terms of performance of their respective functions of teaching, research and extension.

Results of examination, selection of alumni for higher positions in civil service and private management, research papers brought out by faculty and published in reputed journals, the general standing of the faculty and the frequency with which the faculty is called on for policy and similar consultations, the affinity felt by surrounding community for the university and the involvement of the university in programmes of development of the community are some of the indices against which the efficiency of the institution could be judged.

It would be appreciated that there is a tremendous expansion of higher education in the post-independent period in response to the upward pull of the secondary system. Some universities have been established in response to popular demand without ensuring adequate infrastructural facilities. This also applies to the proliferation of colleges, specially in the rural areas. According to some estimates, 40 per cent of the colleges in India could be classified as non-viable. While it would be rash to extend such a judgment to universities, there can be no doubt that there is a gradation in the quality of universities and some of them could not he termed as efficient.

Efficiency of the System of Higher Education. The question of efficiency of the system of higher education is distinct from the question of efficiency of individual institutions. While individual institutions could be operating below optimum level of efficiency, the education system as a whole could be efficient and *vice versa*. Normally the efficiency of systems of higher education would be judged in terms of its contribution to the socio-economic development of the country. Some of the measures are: whether the output of secondary system is being smoothly absorbed into the system of higher education; whether the output of higher education system is being smoothly absorbed in the various tasks of economic development; whether the research output of the university is directly feeding into achieving higher levels of productivity, etc. Considered in this light, the situation may not be perceived to be entirely satisfactory because there are complaints regarding fall in standards of education, inability of the economy to absorb outputs of higher education system, complaints regarding instruction in higher education system not being relevant to the needs of the economy, the continued need for import of technology from abroad, and in general, the dysfunctionality of the output of the higher education system as manifested in the growing number of the educated unemployed, indiscipline and a general, sense of frustration.

These, however, are very large questions and the replies thereto are bound to be diverse and highly relative. We are, therefore, required to reserve judgment on this whole question.

❒

8

Aims of Education

Educational aims in any country have varied with its political, social and economic conditions. The educational system of Greece and Rome raised an issue that is still very important in education today. Should education train good individuals or good citizens? Are the social needs in education more important than the needs of the individual? An individual is born with certain potentialities and natural endowments. It is the task of the educator to develop into a distinct individual. But personality development does not take place in a vacuum. Thus we have to decide whether the individual or the society would occupy the first place in education.

Educators who Emphasis Individual Aim of Education

To enable men to release, to mature, to discipline the human mind and spirit,.... this most influential of all the varieties of energy has always been the task of education. *(John H. Fischer. "The Energies of Education" Education Age, November-December, 1965. P.42 Visual products Division, 3M Company St. Paul Minn).*

Schools exist to help children succeed. *(Gordon Mc. Ctoskey. Education and Public Understanding. New York: Harper & Row. Publishers, Inc. 1958 p. 297).*

Therefore we would ask education to give us men with taste, respect for intelligence, and independence of judgement that will give them confidence to approach the public for what it is a group of distinct individuals, not a lump of reflexes waiting to be conditioned. *(Monroe E. Spaght. The Bright Key. New York: Appleton-Century Crofts, 1965 p. 10).*

In Rigveda, education has been defined as something, which makes a man self-reliant and selfless.

According to Sir Percy Nunn, "Nothing good enters into the human world except in and through the free activities of individual men and women, and that educational practice must be shaped to accord with that truth."

The University Education Commission (1948) speaks about education in these words. "Education according to Indian tradition is initiation into the life of spirit, a training of human soul in the pursuit of truth and the practice of virtue."

Mahatma Gandhi, the father of Basic Education considers education as a means to develop man. He said "By education we mean an all round drawing out of the best in child and man body, mind and spirit".

Aristotre thinks that "Education is the creation of a sound mind in a sound body".

Froebel regards education "As the process through which the child markes internal external".

In the words of Kant "Education is the development in the individual of all the perfection of which he is capable."

Why Stress on Individual Aim

1. The Biologist's Support to Individual Aim of Education. According to Prof. G. Thompson, "Education is for the individual : its function being to enable the individual to survive and live out its complete life. Education is improved to preserve the individual life." Education is given for the sake of the individual save him from destruction. Community exists for the individual, not the individual for the community. Community being the means and individual being the end, education should not set mean over the end. Individual and not society, therefore, should be the centre of all educational efforts and activities.

2. The Naturalists Support to the Individual Aim of Education. The naturalists like Nunn and Rousseau are, of the view that the central aim of education is the autonomous development of the individual. According to Rousseau, "Everything is good as it comes from the hands of Author of Nature, but everything degenerates in the hand of man. God makes all things good. Man meddles with them and they become evil." It is, therefore, that education should be in accordance with the nature of the individual.

3. The Spiritualists Support to Education. The spiritualists are of the view that every individual is a separate entity and responsible for his own actions. Therefore, the main function of education should be to lead the individual to self-realisation. Swami Vivekanand states, "Man is potentially divine. The goal is to manifest this potentiality from within, by controlling nature—external and internal through education."

4. The Psychologists Support to Individual Aim of Education. The psychologists regard each individual a unique one. According to them no two children are identical. The function of education should be to develop the innate powers of the individual so that his maximum development may take place.

5. The Progressivists Support to the Individual Aim of Education. The progressivists hold the view that the progress and advancement of the world is due to great individuals born in different periods of history. It is, therefore, stated by them that the education process should secure condition for the complete development of individuality so that each individual may make his original contribution to the human life.

Criticism of the Individual Aim of Education

1. According to Raymont, an individual is only a figment of imagination. An individual cannot be conceived in isolation from society.
2. The critics of individual aim believe that the individual left to himself is an animal, selfish and indisciplined. The animal instinct of man, if given, a loose reign is sure to lead him to the state of primitive barbarism where the law of jungle prevailed.
3. The exaggerated claim of the individual may have an adverse effect in the politics and economy of a country. The policy of 'Laissezfaire' is not conducive to national interests in the modern times.
4. Absolute freedom to the individual should not be given. The individual may begin to assert that I must have what I want.

Social Aim of Education. The individual is regarded as endowed with a social nature, he is social by instinct. An individual seems everywhere and always to be caught up in an intricate web of social relations. Without them the newborn baby would almost perish. The social process and the educational process are essentially one and the same.

Curriculum is the social stuff out of which the individual realises itself.

Narrow Interpretation of Social Aim of Education. The protagonists of this view think that State is an idealized metaphysical entity over and above the individual citizen, superior in every way. Hence the individual exists for the society. It is, therefore the State that should decide the aim, mode and type of education or training which an individual should receive for its welfare. The Spartan system of education in ancient times and the Nazi system of the recent past reflect this tendency. Undoubtedly such notions played a major role in world conflicts which led to the Two World Wars in 1914 and 1939.

Broader Interpretation of the Social Aim of Education. The Social aim of education finds expression in such concepts as 'education for social service', 'education for citizenship' and education for social efficiency'.

Social Aim in Education

Social aim has been stressed as the supporters of this aim believe that an individual cannot live and develop in isolation from Society. Raymont says that the isolated individual is a figment of the imagination. The individual being a social animal, will be moulded to the needs of the society. The individual will develop through social contacts.

According to John Dewey, social aim in education is stressed as education should make each individual specially efficient and this social efficiency must be achieved by the positive use of individual powers and capacities in social occupations. A socially efficient individual is able to earn his livelihood. He also conforms to moral and social standards of conduct.

Gandhiji formulated the basic scheme with the objective of making public realise that education was not merely for the benefit of the individual but for needs of a predominantly rural and agrarian population.

Limitation of Social Aim in Education

1. Social aim of education envisages the individual as a non-entity and leaves little scope for his personality and unique characteristics to flourish.

2. In recent years there has been a tendency in Western countries among the young people to rebel against the cult of social efficiency. Many students prefer the development and growth of individuality and would want to give up the struggle for social efficiency.

3. Aggression and violence against neighbouring countries have resulted in educational aims of this type. Militant nationalism "my country, right or wrong", are attitudes which may develop in tender minds.

Definitions which Stress Individual and Social Objective of Education:

1. Education is that which increases our ability to enjoy more things more, to live more richly, more creatively, and in greater harmany with ourselves, our environment and our fellowmen. *(Theodore O. Yntema. The Enrichment of Man. The Benjamin Fitirless Memorial Lecture, given, at Carnegie Institute of Technology 65 p. 47).*

2. The main objectives of general education should be two-fold: first to help the student develop those qualities and abilities that will serve him and the community well, no matter what his calling or status in life: and second to foster in him those interests and abilities that will enable him to continue to grow to leant by himself and in whatever joint activity he may be engaged.

3. The goals are to enable each child to play a constructive, respected role in society and to lead a life which to him will be satisfying. *(Educational Policies Commission, American Education and the Search, for Equal Opportunity, Washington, D.C. National Education Association, 1965, p. 17).*

Social and Individual Purposes of Education not Incompatible. 'Social purpose' of education and 'individual purpose' of education are not incompatible terms. The Education Commission 1964-66 has explained the position as, "One of the important principles to be emphasized in the socialistic pattern of society which the nation desires to create is that individual fulfillment will come, not through selfish and narrow loyalties to personal or group interests that through the dedication of all to the wider loyalties of national development in all its parameters."

According to Ross, "Individuality is of no value and personality is a meaningless term apart from the social environment in which they are development and made manifest. Self-realization can be achieved only through social service and social ideas of real value can come into being only through free individuals who have developed valuable individuality. The circle cannot be broken."

The individual and the society, both be regarded as realities, neither of the two being absolutely independent of the other. Instead of being regarded as isolated entities, the individual and the society should be considered as functionally related to each other. The individual acting on the society, and the society reacting on the individual. The individual is the product of society which the society in its own turn finds its advancement in the development of its individual members. In the words of John Adam, "Individuality requires a social medium to grow. Without social contacts we are not human."

Democratic and Totalitarian Aims in Education

Educational aims in any country have varied with its social economic and geographical conditions. In recent past political system has been the dominating factor in determining the aims and ideals of education. The two systems which are considered here in relation to aims in education will be democratic and the totalitarian.

Aims of Education in the Totalitarian and Democratic States

Both use educational systems as a direct means of economic development.

Both use educational systems as a conscious means of transforming their society.

Both lay great stress on vocational skills to bring about economic efficiency.

Both make all out attempts to provide schooling for all. An attack on mass illiteracy is a must.

State Control of Education in a Totalitarian State. The child in a totalitarian state is educated not only exclusively by the state but ultimately exclusively for the state as well. Thus the state comes to assume ethical as well as political sovereignty in the education of its wards. The state organizes and maintains schools for its own. The teachers in a totalitarian state must propagate and indoctrinate the decisions made by higher ups. As in the army, the schools of a totalitarian state will emphasize drill and obedience at the expense of initiative and criticism.

The merits and demerits of such an educational philosophy are the same as those of the political theory after which it is patterned. Thus the aims and ideals of education depend upon the philosophy that prevails in a society. In the mid-twentieth century, Japan and Nazi regimes stressed that education should produce patriotic citizens who would fight to expand the territories of their nation's superiority. The cultural revolution in China in the 1960's was directed towards the ideals set by the totalitarian state.

In a totalitarian state, pupils are not encouraged to look critically at the problems and evils existing in society. They may be content with the *status quo*. Passive acceptance of the country's political, economic and other policies will grow in the minds of the students. Militant nationalism, "My country, right or wrong" are attitudes which may develop in tender minds. Aggression and violence against neighbouring countries have resulted in educational aims of this type.

Aims of education in a totalitarian state may be enumerated as under:

1. Each individual must be trained to subordinate his interests to the interests of the state.
2. Every child must undergo a rigorous code of discipline.
3. The student is made to realize the value and importance of obedience and conformity.
4. Thinking along the lines approved by the authorities is stressed. Very little independent thinking is allowed.
5. Physical education and military training are given great importance.

Education in a Democracy. Since every individual counts in a democracy, it enjoins that every person be always treated as an end. A man is to be educated as man because of his humane nature no matter whether he is high born or low, and no matter what the economic condition of his parents is. Nothing less than universal education will suffice. Education is conditioned by deep regard for civic responsibilities; emphasis on hard work, dignity of labour, initiative, enterprise reliance etc. Since all men in a democracy are free, education must be free, that is there must be no economic barriers to its acquisition. Since in a democracy all men are politically free, all should have a liberal education.

Following will be the aims of education in a democratic set up:

1. It should develop a wide range of wholesome interests in each pupil by providing for learning through cooperative work.
2. It should develop social outlook.
3. It should develop the capacity of the pupil to sift truth from false-hood, fact from propaganda and to reject the dangerous appeal of fanaticism and prejudice.
4. It should develop ability of constructive and independent thinking.
5. It should provide for the training in dignity of labour.
6. It should provide equal opportunities for all.
7. It should develop love and respect for others. It should develop human relations.
8. It should cater to the individual differences of children and teach them accordingly. No attempt should be made towards uniformity.
9. It should develop a passion for social justice based upon sensitiveness to the social evils and exploitation of the weak.
10. Vocational choices are broad based.
11. It encourages originally and inventiveness.

State Control of Education in a Welfare State Like India. It is generally believed that neither a policy of complete *Laissez faire* nor of complete state control of education is suited in a Welfare State. The state must take positive as well as negative action to maintain a proper balance of social welfare for its citizens. The state must step forward and ensure not only an adequate amount of education but also education of an adequately high standard.

The degree of State control of education has varied from state to state at different times. Prof, John S. Burbacher outlines the position as, "At one time all education was under private supervision, latterly, more and more of it has come under the government. In some places the government merely provides the school building and teacher. In other it goes further and offers free text books and supplies. In still others, it furnishes such services as medical care, transportation to and from school and noon day lunches. Probably no one today would like to see the government abandon any of these services."

Analytical Meaning of Education

Education is the Harmonious Development of Child. Education is the harmonious development of the child. Through education all aspects—physical, mental, spiritual and moral are developed.

Education is a Dynamic Process. Education is a dynamic and progressive process. It reconstructs a new and better social pattern according to the changing needs of time, place and society.

Education is the Development of Innate and Acquired Powers of the Child. Every child has innate capacities. Education helps in developing those natural qualities of the child. It provides every person with the opportunity of developing according to his capacities.

Education is a Life Long Process. It starts in mother's womb and ends in tomb. The sequence of learning through experiences goes on up to death.

Education is a Process of Adjustment with the Environment. Education helps the individual in making adjustment with his own self, parents, peers and society etc.

Western thinkers have given following definitions:

According to **Aristotle,** "Education is the creation of a sound mind in a sound body." Aristotle has regarded the meaning of education complete by mentioning physical and spiritual development.

According to **T.P. Nunn,** "Education is the complete development of individuality so that man can make an original contribution to human life according to his best capacity."

According to **Frobel,** "Education is unfoldment of what is already enfolded in the seed. It is the process through which a child expresses his internal abilities."

Nunn and James have also stressed individual and social development but their definitions are vague.

According to **Dewey,** "Education is the development of all those capacities in the individual which enable him to control his environment and fulfil his possibilities."

According to **James,** "Education is the organisation of acquired habits of such action as will fit the individual to his physical and social environment."

According to **Pestalozzi,** "Education is the natural, harmonious and progressive development of man's innate powers". Pestalozzi has talked about the development of innate powers whereas education also brings about personal, social, moral, cultural, economic, national and international development.

According to **Bossing,** "The function of education is conceived to be the adjustment of man to his environment, to the end that the most enduring satisfaction may accrue to the individual and to the society."

After studying the interpretation given by various educationists, we can classify the meaning of education into two categories—Narrower and Broader. In the narrow sense, education is regarded as equivalent to instruction, imparted in school or college. Education is believed to begin with the entrance of a child to the school and end with his departure from the university. Education includes those specific influences which are brought to bear upon the child with a definite purpose in a pre-planned, suitable, and methodical manner, by parents, teachers and other members of the community, for the preservation of the cultural heritage. According to this view education is limited to classroom teaching and readymade materials. Education is given in a formal way, under set and controlled conditions and environment. It is pre-planned and is given by teachers in the classroom.

According to **J.S. Mill,** education in its narrower sense means, "The culture which each generation purposely gives to its successor in order to qualify, to keep up and to improve the level attained. Thus education becomes a purposeful activity which is planned deliberately for the purpose of the child's individual and social development. This activity is organised through the school as the chief agency of education."

According to **Lodge,** "In the wider sense, all experiences are said to be educative. Even the bite of mosquito and the taste of water melon experiences have a directly educative effect on us." The child educates his parents, the pupils educate their teacher. Everything that we say, think or do educates us.

In this wider sense life is education and education is life. Whatever broadens our horizon, deepens our insight, refines our reactions and stimulates our thoughts and feelings educates us. Life is a long process of education and education is synonymous with the act of living.

Education of Modern Indian Society

After independence, democratic view point was adopted. At that time education made its contribution and tried to bring prosperity in country. According to Rajendra Prasad, "India has to choose for herself a culture that derives inspiration from what is noble in our ancient culture and at the same time does not ignore the demands of the present age."

Aims of Education According to University Education Commission, 1948

Pandit Nehru had observed, "Great changes have taken place in the country and the educational system must also be in keeping with them. The entire basis of education must be revolutionised."

According to University Education Commission, 1948, the aims of education are as follows:

(a) Development of leadership.

(b) Preservation and transfer of culture.

(c) Vocational efficiency.

(d) Development of democratic qualities in school.

(e) Emphasis on human and spiritual training.

(f) Character development.

Aims of Education According to Secondary Education Commission, 1952-53

This commission has stated that education which is national in character must develop in its citizens habits, attitudes and qualities of character and equip them to bear the burden of life in the changing economic structure.

According to Secondary Education Commission aims of education are as follows:

(a) Development of democratic citizenship.

(b) Development of sense of patriotism.

(c) Development of vocational efficiency.

(d) Development of personality.

(f) Development of leadership.

Development of Democratic Citizenship. It is a challenging responsibility with education to carefully train every citizen for democratic citizenship. Such a training develops following qualities:

(a) ***Clear Thinking.*** A democratic citizen should have the understanding and the intellectual integrity to distinguish truth from falsehood and facts from propaganda. Education should train the child for this purpose.

(b) ***Clearness in Speech and Writing.*** This quality is essential for successful living in democracy which is based not on force but on free discussion and persuasion.

(c) ***Receptivity to New Ideas.*** Education must aim at broadening the intellectual horizon of young scholars to enable them to accept new ideas that can help in strengthening democratic forces.

Development of Sense of Patriotism. Another important aim which the secondary school must foster is the development of a sense of true patriotism. True patriotism involves a sense of appreciation of the social and cultural achievements, a readiness to recognize its weaknesses and an earnest desire to serve one's country.

Development of Personality. Education should develop literary, artistic and cultural interests of the students. These are necessary for self-expression and for the full development of human personality. For this purpose subjects like art, craft, music, dance etc. should be included in the scheme of studies.

Development of Vocational Efficiency. Education must aim at increasing the productive or vocational efficiency of young students.

Aims of Education According to Indian Education Commission, 1964-66

According to Dr. Radhakrishnan, "It is my earnest desire that the Commission should survey all aspects of educational system at all levels and give suggestions that may help the educational system in progressing at all levels."

According to Kothari Commission, "One of the important social objectives of education is to equalise opportunity, enabling the backward or underprivileged classes and individuals to use education as a tool for improvement of their social and economic condition".

The most important and urgent reform needed in education is to transform it, to relate it to the life, needs and aspirations of the people and thereby make a powerful instrument of social, economic and cultural transformation, necessary for realization of the national goals. For this purpose the commission has suggested the following objectives of education:

(a) Increasing productivity.

(b) Social and national integration.

(c) Acceleration the process of modernisation.

(d) Developing social, moral and spiritual values.

These objectives are discussed below.

Education for Increasing Productivity. Though India is a land of vast resources, yet it has not become self-sufficient. For this purpose, the resources must be exploited and education must be related to productivity to increase national income. In order to create a link between education and productivity the following programme has been suggested by Kothari Commission:

Science Education. Science education must become an integral part of school education and ultimately some study of science should become a part of all courses in the humanities and social sciences at university stage also. The quality of science teaching must also be improved considerably so as to promote a deep understanding of basic principles, to develop problem solving and analytical skills and to promote the spirit of enquiry and experimentation.

Work Experience. In the programme of relating education to life and productivity, work experience must be introduced as an integral part of all education general and vocational. To commission work experience implies participation in productive work in school, in the home, in a workshop, on a farm, in a factory or in any productive situation. All purposeful education should include study of languages, humanities and social sciences, study of mathematics and natural sciences, work experience and social services.

Work experience is a method of integrating education with work. In the present education system work experience and social services have almost been totally neglected. Along with other elements of education work experience should be greately emphasised for the following reasons:

(a) It will bridge the gap between intellectual and manual work.

(b) It will relate education to productivity and also as a means of social and national integration.

(c) It will decrease the over academic nature of formal education.

(d) It will make the entry of youth into the world of work and employment easier by enabling them to adjust themselves to it.

Vocationalisation. Every attempt should be made to give a vocational bias to secondary education and to increase the emphasis on agricultural and technological education at the university stage. This will surely bring education into closer relationship with productivity. In the modern Indian society which is heading towards industrialisation, it is essential to considerably expand professional education at the university stage, especially in agricultural and technological fields.

Education for National Integration. India is a land of diverse social groups. Unity and harmony among these groups is the basis of national integration. Social and national integration is an important objective of a national system of education. The Commission has suggested the following steps for strengthening the nation through education.

The Common School System. The present educational system in our country instead of bringing social groups and classes together is tending to increase social segregation and class distinctions. The schools for the masses (generally maintained by the government) are of poorer quality than those run by private bodies. Good schools are not within the reach of a common man's pocket. This is one of the major weaknesses of the existing educational system. In the opinion of the Commission, "If our educational system is to become a powerful instrument of national development in general, and social and national integration in particular, we must march toward the goal of a Common School System of public education." The common school must be opened to all children irrespective of caste, creed, community and economic or social status.

— It should charge no tuition fee.

— It should maintain a good standard of education in order to meet the needs of average parents so that they may not ordinarily feel the need of sending their children to other expensive schools.

Social and National Service. Social and national service should be made obligatory for all students at all stages. It should form an integral part of education at secondary school and university levels. This programme will prove an effective instrument for building character improving discipline, inculcating a faith in the dignity of labour and developing a sense of social responsibility, if it is organised concurrently with academic studies in schools and colleges. The following are the main forms of organising such a programme:

(a) At the primary stage this programme should be developed in all schools on the lines of Basic Education.

(b) At the lower secondary stage social service should be made compulsory for all students for thirty days a year, at the higher secondary for twenty days and at the under-graduate stage it should be made obligatory for all students or sixty days a year, to be done in one or more stretches. Every educational institution should develop a programme of social and community service of its own in which all students must be involved for the periods as indicated above.

(c) Labour and social service camps or N.C.C. should be organised in each district as alternative forms of such service for those students for whom no other programmes of social service have been organised in their own institutions.

Promoting National Consciousness

India is a land of different castes, peoples, communities, languages, religions and cultures. The main role of our schools, colleges and universities should, therefore, be to enable our students to discover 'unity in diversity' and in this way, foster a sense of national solidarity and national consciousness among them. This can be done by:

Democratic Values. The educational programme in schools and colleges should be designed to inculcate democratic values, such as scientific temper of mind, tolerance, respect for the culture of other national groups etc. This will enable our young citizens to adopt democracy not only as a form of government but also as a way of life.

The Promotion of Understanding and Re-evaluation of Our Cultural Heritage. This can be achieved by the well-organised teaching of language and literature, philosophy, religion and history of India and by introducing the students to Indian architecture, sculpture, painting, music, dance and drama. Holiday camps and summer schools on inter-state basis, can also be organised fruitfully, for breaking down regional and linguistic barriers.

Creation of a strong faith in the future towards would involve an attempt to bring home to the students, the principles of the constitution, the great human values, referred to in its preamble, the nature of the democratic and socialistic society.

Education for International Understanding. There is no contradiction between national consciousness and developing international understanding. Schools should promote international outlook through the study of humanities and social sciences, simultaneously with developing national consciousness.

Education for Modernisation

In a modern society stock of knowledge is far greater, the pace of its growth is infinitely quicker and social change is very rapid. This needs a radical change in the educational system. Education in a modern society is no longer concerned mainly with the imparting of knowledge or the preparation of a finished product but with the awakening of curiosity, the development of proper interests, attitudes and values and the building up of such essential skills as independent study and capacity to think and judge for oneself, without which it is not possible to become a responsible member of a democratic society. Therefore the process of modernisation will be directly related to the pace of educational advance. Education brings modernisation in following ways:

(a) The way to modernise quickly is to spread education.

(b) By producing educated and skilled citizens.

(c) By bringing a radical change in the method of teaching and in the training of teachers.

(d) By training an adequate and competent intelligentsia.

Education for Social, Moral and Spiritual Values

The expanding knowledge and the growing power which it places at the disposal of modern society must be combined with the strengthening and deepening of the sense of social responsibility and a keener appreciation of moral and spiritual values. For this purpose, active measures should be adpoted to give a value-orientation to education. These measures are:

(a) The central and state Governments should introduce education in moral, social and spiritual values in all institutions.

(b) The privately managed institutions should also follow the same steps.

(c) University department should undertake preparation of special literature for this purpose by students and teachers.

(d) For this purpose, a syllabus giving well chosen information about each of the major religions, should be included as a part of the course in citizenship or general education to be introduced in schools and colleges.

(e) Some periods should be set apart in the time table for this purpose.

We may say that education is the most vital force which can help in the realisation of national objectives. While keeping in view the best features of the modern European culture and civilization, the Commission did not ignore the essential characteristics of our ancient culture and civilization as well as the needs and aspirations of our present day society. It is for the first time that we have been given an integrated picture of Indian education in all its wide and diverse dimensions. We need not copy the western models blindly. And thus consequently suffer the loss of inspiration.

Some of the most important individual aims of education are:

1. The Knowledge Aim. Knowledge is power. Achievements of all kinds are made possible only through knowledge. An ignorant man can do nothing for himself or for anyone else; and is like an animal. Knowledge is basic for living a rich and happy life. It is for this reason that many educationists consider imparting of knowledge to the people as an important aim. That is why all the schools have graded syllabus for children of different ages and classes. Different subjects are taught in the schools as different aspects of knowledge. In fact acquisition of knowledge is the nucleon around which most of the activities of the schools in the whole world revolve. Most of the teaching strategies developed for teaching aim at imparting knowledge alone. The examination systems in all countries measure, by and large, only knowledge. In fact, education and knowledge giving have become synonymous. Teachers, students and parents all think that good education and good schools are only those which make their children knowledgeable.

There is no doubt that knowledge-giving should be considered an important aim of education. In the past many philosophers like Plato, Aristotle, the Sophists and many others emphasised this aim very much. Comenius said that an ideal school should impart knowledge of all subjects to all men and women. Knowledge and intellectual development go together; and cultivation of intelligence is an importance of education according to Bertrand Russel. Bacon's slogan was "all knowledge for all", knowledge was virtue for Socrates. To Cicero knowledge was a means of mental development. Even the development of other aspects of human personality is dependent largely on acquisition of knowledge. Thus, it is an important aim of education to impart knowledge. But where are we wrong?

We commit a serious error when we accept and say that it is the only aim of education, when we say that nothing else is important. Knowledge alone is not enough and sufficient for living a happy and complete life. Knowledge is a tool which has to be used for achieving many more things. So these many more things should also be brought within the purview of aims of education. Hence, the right way is to say that among many aims of education, knowledge aim is also very important.

2. Harmonious Development Aim. It means harmonious development of child's personality. Child's personality is one word but many things. Intellectual and cognitive development is one aspect. Emotional development including emotional control is another. Feelings, attitudes, interests, values etc., also fall within this component of emotional development. Similarly, development of skills, desirable habits and actions constitute still another aspect of personality development. Adjustment to the environment and many social behaviours come under this. Equal development of all these aspects, balanced development of these, is considered an aim of education. If it happens that a person is very knowledgeable, but socially maladjusted, this would mean a lap-sided development of the personality.

3. Vocational Aim. This is also known as the 'bread-and-butter" aim of education. Thus no doubt should be considered an important aim of education. It simply means that education received by an individual should enable him to earn his bread, should enable him to get a job, some work that pays him sufficient money regularly so that the individual is able to buy bread, clothes, house, and other things necessary for living a decent and comfortable life. This has led in many countries, to a slogan by the people and educators which is "job-oriented education". Vocationalization of education is another dimension of the same. Gandhiji's basic education concept had this implication. When he said that true education should be, for the boys and girls, a kind of insurance against employment, he meant to emphasize vocational aim of education.

Again, although we all accept that vocational aim is very important, yet we commit a mistake when we say that it is the only aim to which education should cater. We should always think that along with vocational aim there are other aims which are equally important. We should neither ignore or belittle the importance of vocational aim, nor we should consider this only important aim. Nehru struck the balance between vocational and cultural aims of education when he said that cultural and vocational or productive aspects of education both are essential. "Everybody should be a producer as well as a good citizen and not a sponge on another person," said he. Mahatma Gandhi also emphasized the same point when he said that body, mind and spirit all should be developed by education. Although many philosophers from the ancient times to the present day have insisted upon the satisfaction of the soul belittling the importance of vocation in life, yet their view can not be the conscious of opinion. These should be taken as the extreme views and one-sided opinions. The majority of the people in the world feel that education should make individual self-dependent and capable of earning their livelihood.

4. Aesthetic Aim. This aim emphasizes that education should develop in the pupil an aesthetic sense which means a taste for good and beautiful things. They feel that excellence of taste and fairness of feeling can form the basis of good character and genuine morality. By developing in the child sensitivity to what is beautiful and excellent ideals may be generated which play an important role in being a moral person. Aesthetic development is, in fact, a part of the education of the whole man. It is a sort of emotional training. In the past the Athenians considered this important. They aimed, through education, to develop a well-rounded individual, one whose physical, moral, intellectual and aesthetic powers were developed. For developing aesthetic sense of the child the educators stressed that while teaching pupils love of beauty and art should be fostered. The students should be presented with a large variety of art forms such as paintings, drawings, beautiful sceneries both real and painted, songs, poetry, etc.

5. The Moral Aim. This aim lays stress on the ethical development of the people. Character-formation and learning of social and moral values are the focus of this aim. Gandhiji termed this as "purity of heart". Vivekananda's "man-making" function of education also means the same thing. Dewey said "all education forms character—moral and mental". This, in other words, means emphasizing the moral aim of education. Raymont also considered "cultivation of strength and purity of character" as an important aim of education. Herbart said "the whole work of education could be summed up in the concept of morality." All the idealist philosophers supported the moral aim as an ultimate aim of education. National Policy on Education of 1986 also said that education should be made a "forceful tool for the cultivation of social and moral values".

There can be no gain saying that education should teach morality to children. It is an universally accepted aim of education. But, the difficulty with this aim is how to define character and morality, what are its behavioural components, are these behavioural components acceptable universally, does morality help the individual in actual situations of life, is there any standard way of teaching morality. These questions have no set and unambiguous answers. Morality is good, but very difficult to be taught, particularly in today's materialistic world. Yet, the aim cannot be scored out simply for these difficulties. In a democratic country where the assumption is that the human being is perfect and given the freedom he will make the best use of it in the interest of the society and his own interest, it becomes still more important to teach morality to people.

6. Complete Living Aim. This aim means that education should enable the individuals to live a life which is full and complete. In other words it means preparing the individuals for life. Living a full and complete life means exercising and using all capacities and abilities in the interest of one's well-being. Keeping good health, developing a sound mind and using it for the benefit of life's amenities, enjoying life and enriching it culturally, living like a good citizen and gainfully employed may be considered some important features of full or complete living. In other words it is the same as harmonious development of personality. According to this aim education should enable the individual to carry out all necessary activities of life successfully. He should be an enlightened citizen and an efficient man. Herbert Spencer seems to be the advocate of this aim. It is in a way laying an emphasis on liberal education which emphasizes teaching the pupils everything that is needed in life. It may be termed as life-centred education or education for life.

The main difficulty with this aim is how to define "completeness of life". When is life complete? Even it is possible to define completeness of life it becomes more difficult to identify what will make it so.

❒

9

Women Education

In the past no importance was attached to the education of girls. In the beginning of the present century the percentage of literate women was only 0.8. The enrolment in the primary schools was 12 for every 100 boys and that in the secondary schools it was 4 for every 100. The total enrolment in the colleges was 26,474.

The two problems of women's education that attracted the attention of educational commissions were :

(*a*) backwardness.

(*b*) slow progress.

As early as 1882 the Hunter Commission said that the female education in the country had been till then in a very backward condition and recommended for an over-all improvement in the condition. It recommended that more grants should be given to girls schools and that moneys should be spent in equitable proportion on girls and boys schools.

To encourage girls education the commission recommended for a liberal scheme of scholarships to girls, a provision of facilities for their professional training and opening of secondary schools.

In spite of valuable recommendations made by commissions and committees on female education, at the beginning of the present century there was hardly any provision for the formal schooling of girls. It was only after 1901 when women came out of homes to shoulder responsibility in the struggle for freedom, that we see a progress in the field of the education of girls.

During the first half of this century much faster progress was made. The education for women expended enormously. Their status in the society got raised. A few aspects of the phenomenal growth in female education are given below:

1. The rate of expansion of female education was higher than that among the boys.
2. The enrolment at the primary stage increased from 12 for 100 boys in 1901 to 39 for 100 in 1950.
3. The enrolment at the secondary stage increased from 4 for 100 boys in 1901 to 15 for 100 in 1950.
4. The enrolment in the university rose from 264 in 1901 to 40,000 in 1950.
5. The education in mixed schools was more in the primary classes than in the secondary classes.

But there was still a very wide gulf between the education for boys and that for the girls. It was specially hinted at by the National Committee on Education of Women under the chairmanship of Smt. Durgabai Deshmukh (1958-59). The Committee pointed out that the government did not realise even as late as 1958 that the problem of female education was a special one and as such it failed to provide necessary funds for the rapid development of women's education for which a suggestion had been given as early as 1882.

The National Committee on Women Education suggested that the education of women should be regarded as a major programme in education for some years to come and that special schemes should be prepared for this purpose and funds needed to work them out should be provided on a priority basis. The committee also suggested the setting up of a special machinery at the state as well as at the Central level to look after the education of women.

The problem of wide disparity between the education of boys and girls at all stages and in all sectors of education is really one that claims urgent solution. The Education Commission has stressed the need for solving this problem at an early date. It remarked that had the problem been given due attention right from the beginning the need for special programmes as suggested by the Durgabai Deshmukh Committee would have not arisen at all. We must therefore try to bridge the gulf between the education of boys and girls at all stages primary, secondary and higher, and in all sectors of education.

The next Committee for the development of female education was the one which was headed by, Hansa Mehta. The Committee discussed the problem of differentiation of curriculum between boys and girls. The Hunter Commission had recommended in 1882 that curriculum for girls should be different from what it is for boys as the instruction which is useful for a boy may not be useful for a girl. The Committee under the Chairmanship of Hansa Mehta made the following recommendations.

(a) There should be no need to differentiate curricula on the basis of sex in a democratic socialistic society.

(b) In the transitional period we should accept certain psychological differences between the two sexes and we may build curricula in such a way that these differences are given due importance but care should be exercised not to perpetuate them.

The problem of differentiation of curricula for boys and girls has been already discussed under section 12.9 in detail and hence need not be repeated here.

There has been appointed one more committee which studied the problem of women's education in 6 states under the chairmanship of Shri M. Bhaktvatsalam. It had surveyed the education of girls and concluded that the education has been very poorly developed so far.

Three aspects of female education stand out as follows :

(a) problem concerning expansion of women's education.

(b) problem of higher education of girls.

(c) problem of professional education of girls and married women.

The problem concerning expansion has been very carefully examined by the National Committee on Women's Education (1958-59). So far as the expansion of primary education is concerned, the number of girls enrolled for every 100 boys is about 50 now. At the middle school stage the gap is still wider. The Constitutional Directive could not be fulfilled even by the end of 1980 even we if proceeded at a faster rate in the field of expansion of women's education. We will have to educate public opinion to overcome traditional prejudices against girls education. We will have to encourage girls education by providing free text-books, writing materials and even clothing. We would have to make mixed schools popular at the primary stage and shall have to open separate schools for girls at the middle and secondary school stage wherever they are needed and it is possible to open them. Girls are more useful than boys at home.

Hence, they tend to be withdrawn earlier. Public opinion is still not in favour of extending education among girls to higher stages. Hence a large portion of girls have to leave school early. For girls who leave the primary stage at about the age 14 and get married, it is proposed that part-time or full-time courses should be organised in homescience or the household industries like tailoring, arts and crafts, poultry and dairying so that they may prepare themselves better for their future life as housewives and mothers.

At the secondary stage, special programmes will have to be initiated for girls who intend to join secondary schools. In 1950-51 the proportion of the enrolment of the girls to that of the boys was about 1:6 in middle and 1:6.5 in higher secondary schools. By 1980 it had been raised to 1:2 in middle schools and 1:3 in higher secondary ones. Special efforts shall have to be still made to achieve targets set. Either more separate schools will have to be opened or where it is not possible to do so, women teachers will have to be kept on the staff. Women's hostels or subsidised transport shall have to be provided. Encouragement shall have to be given in the form of scholarships and free education.

Problem of Training and Employment

The Indian society is undergoing a change. Woman is adopting her own career. Her age of marriage is rising. Her role outside the home is becoming an important aspect of the social and economic life of the country. The role of woman outside the home will assume still larger significance in time to come. There is a problem of unemployment among educated girls. It is therefore necessary to pay special attention to the problems of training and employment.

The 1961 Census showed that about a million young educated women above the age of 24, though matriculates, were working simply as housewives. The 1971 Census presented even more dismal picture. How horrible is it to lay waste their powers which could be profitably used for national reconstruction and development! There is a need for training and employing them in nation-building activities.

As the marriage age among girls rises, the number of young unmarried women becomes larger. A suitable career has to be singled out for pursuit before a girl gets married. Then again after marriage, when she becomes almost free from home-making activities and when her children reach a school going age, she needs some employment. The time at her disposal before she is married is to be used in some part-time job and the time after marriage when she is free has to be used in full-time work. Teaching, nursing, and social service are some of the areas in which part or full-time jobs can be secured for women. Hence, there is a need for training girls for these services.

Women Polytechnics

In all polytechnics courses of special interest to girls should be developed. A few such courses that have been started for women in 17 polytechnics spread all over the country are courses in:

(a) secretarial practice.

(b) pharmacy.

(c) interior decoration.

(d) electronics and radio technology.

(e) commercial art.

(f) dress making.

(g) instrument technology.

(h) architecture.

(i) medical laboratory technology.

(j) library science.

These courses are being offered at certificate are levels. Efforts should be made to attract into them girls who have just passed the middle or high school examination. More women polytechnics need opening. It is suggested that if guidance services are amply provided to school leavers at the high school stage and if the Principals of women polytechnics associate themselves with the headmistresses and Principals of higher secondary schools more girls may be attracted to these careers.

Women Polytechnics : Agricultural. A large number of girls in rural areas may be attracted to supporting services needed by a farmer. There are many trades which are based upon agriculture. At the post-matriculation stage, opportunities for giving vocational education in agriculture may be provided on a sufficiently large scale. Courses of special interest to girls will have to be devised and developed in agricultural polytechnics. For example; courses in applied nutrition, dairying, animal husbandry, poultry farming are most suitable for matriculate girls. Besides, there is an urgent need for such courses in the country; for instance, in the present circumstances, we have to change our dietary habits and such courses may help a great deal in meeting food shortage. Women in rural households can safely manage these affairs. A network of agricultural polytechnics may be set up to provide girls vocational education in courses referred to above.

Higher Education for Women

We do not subscribe to the opinion that it is no longer necessary to give a special attention to higher education of women since they are taking its advantage fully. To begin with, it must be emphasised that there exists an acute shortage of educated women to shoulder directional and organisational responsibilities in many professions and occupations. For example, there is a great demand of highly educated women workers in a series of occupational fields, such as nutrition, dietetics, institutional management, etc. Specially vigorous efforts have yet to be made to expand women's education at the university level.

Considering the changing needs of the Indian society and the requirements of national development, a still greater expansion of higher education has become imperative. During the decade 1950-1960 the proportion of women students in colleges and universities to the total enrolment was raised from 13 percent to 21. In the following decade it came about 30 percent: but there is an urgent need to raise it up to 40 percent at least. For the healthy growth of higher education among womenfolk the following programmes have been suggested by the Education Commission:

1. a programme of financial assistance and scholarships to women students in colleges and universities on a liberal scale.

2. a programme of suitable but economical hostel facilities for women on a large scale.

3. a free access to courses in arts, humanities, sciences and technology.

The first two programmes are self explanatory. The National Council for Women's Education appointed a committee under the chairmanship of Smt. Hansa Mahta. The committee recommended that courses available for women should not be strictly compartmentalised, implying that women should not in any case be compelled to take up a particular course. The Committee gave a warning that if choice is restricted to women it shall be wrong in national interest. The Education Commission also did not like that girls should be forced to take up particular courses only. It suggested that the more academic type of girls with ambitions of pursuing careers of research or teaching at the college or university level or in professions such as medicine and technology should have all the opportunities and incentives for doing so.

The most popular professions for women are nursing and education. Facilities for higher education in these areas have to be strengthened. At the B.Sc. level in some universities Nursing has been introduced with a view to preparing qualified nursing staff. A scientific and professional course needs development so that it may have an academic value besides leading to a higher level of professional training in nursing. Similarly, there is a need to vitalise and upgrade the courses in Education at B.A. level which have been introduced in eleven universities. Women decide earlier whether they would adopt teaching as their profession or not. Hence it is necessary that either the courses in Education at B.A. level be so prepared that women opting for them may be directly employable in teaching or concurrent integrated courses in general and professional teacher education may be given to them to enable them to join teaching at an earlier age.

Higher education for women must be linked up with avenues of employment because in the absense of employment their education will be wasted away. Hence, specific avenues will have to be searched out where their services may be utilised fruitfully. The services of highly educated women are needed in education, social work and nursing and similar professional fields. Their services are also required in nutrition, dietetics, institutional management and similar occupational areas. Home science has been recognised as an academic discipline in as many as 33 universities. A woman who takes up this subject at the university level should be so equipped that she may be able to work in professional fields of dietetics, food technology, family welfare work, extension work in community development and Welfare Extension Projects. She must be able to take up research work in projects end schemes of I.C.M.R., I.C.A.R., and Council of Child Welfare.

Co-education

Co-education is the education of boys and girls together in the same institution, admission being secured on equal terms and opportunities being offered for the mixing of both the sexes in all the activities cannected with the institution. It does not mean admission of boys and girls into each other's institutions with no opportunities of mutual contacts in connection with the school activities. Co-education therefore, means education of the children of both the sexes in the same institution with fuller freedom of mixing with each other freely.

Much has been said on the vexed question of co-education without any body as yet saying the conclusive word on it. It has been as much a perplexing problem in the West as it is in India. Its history in india is of a recent origin. We do not come across any references from our ancient culture about education. Our ancestors were against this institution. But the practice of co-education in the West is quite old. There was co-education in ancient Greece and Rome. Pestalozzi considered it as quite useful. Even in France, it was found practicable. As a matter of convenience, as a measure of financial economy and as a result of the belief that boys and girls have much to gain, mixed schools have gradually gained importance and increased in number. Co-education in the real sense obtains in America and U.S.S.R. In England, Italy and Germany, co-education is mainly confined to the primary and college stages. There general opinion is against secondary stage.

How Far is it Desirable

In India it has remained in the nature of a problem. In the other countries co-education is a favoured idea. Is co-education a really immoral institution, resulting in gross corruption and criminal sexual laxity, spoiling the students completely or is it one of the most beneficial institutions the crying need of our country, the panacea of all evil, the only psychologically sound method of imparting education and removing the false sexological complexes?

There is no doubt that much can be said in favour of co-education psychologically. It is true enough that the establishment of normal relationships between boys and girls and the growth or familiarity between them would make them develop more naturally and would remove much of false shyness, abnormal and unnatural behaviour and would lead to a better understanding between boys and girls. Greater contact between boys and girls will, no doubt, result in a sense of comradeship and after due course of time will be able to approach each other without giving that undue emphasis to the sexual aspect.

Competition amongst boys and girls would lead to greater efficiency. This is supported by the results of examinations in the United States of America where full scope is given to co-education at all stages primary, secondary and university. Co-education also tones up the discipline of the institution because the presence of the opposite sex has a wholesome effect on their morals. Boys become less coarse and vulgar and girls less shy and morbid. An eminent educationist once said, "I would advise the education of sexes together. Segregation is unhealthy and stirs the sex urge. I can guarantee nothing in a school where there are girls alone." There is some truth in it.

Co-education would engender good social contacts between the two sexes. They would be relieved of mental strain and a better social development would take place. Both would develop natural and rational personalities.

Co-education would suit a poor country like ours. There shall be a good deal of saving. Duplication of buildings, staff and other establishment expenses would be avoided. Co-education would be economical.

Advantages of Co-education

Co-education is as much a fascinating problem as it is vexing. It has both advantages and disadvantages.

1. It is psychologically very sound. The repressed feelings of both sexes find healthy and congenial environments. It would remove false complexes of both boys and girls.

2. The mixing of the sexes is natural as the feminine mind gains from association with boys and vica versa.

3. It is most economical. We cannot afford to have separate medical, industrial and technical institutions.

4. Co-education will lead to greater literacy.

5. Students can study the characteristics of the opposite sex. Pope has said, "The proper study of mankind is man."

6. Most of the marriages made after co-educational experience are successful.

7. General morals and character are also built.

8. Well integrated personalities are developed.

9. It will bring about saner attitude for each other. The boys will learn to respect girls and vice-versa. Better understanding will take place.

10. Co-education will lead to healthy compelition in studies and co-curricular activities.

11. In view of the growing demand for general education and lack of separate institutions co-education is the only solution of the problem.

12. Co-education will reduce mental diseases. Dr. Freud believed that co-education alone could keep young people free from certain dieases of mind.

13. Better demestic life would be developed through co-education. Addition once said, "Female friendship is necessary for intellectual development."

Disadvantages of Education

Let us consider the other side of the medal as well. Every rose has thorns with it. Every smile is accompanied by a tear. Wherever co-education has so many merits, it has demerits also.

1. In all cases of repression, whenever freedom is gained all of a sudden, the result is always riot which, though it lasts for a short while, can never be avoided.

2. Their vocations in life are different and this points out to the need of totally different types of education for them. The task of propagation of the race, bringing up children and building the nation has to be done by women, while men will have to do the roughest business. To encourage co-education would be silly.

3. Co-education would mean the same type of education for both men and women. And men and women are temperamentally different and education, therefore must in their cases be different from each other.

4. Mixing of sexes at the adolescent stage when sex urge is at its highest pitch, is not advisable. It distracts the attention of both boys and girls and hampers their progress in studies.

5. There are some subjects which cannot be taught together especially biology and poetry.

6. Co-education institutions are difficult to organise and manage and there is a good deal of truth in it. It will create many problems of discipline.

7. The result of the impact of each other's personality would be that girls will become masculine and boys effeminate.

8. Under a uniform code of discipline, girls are likely to suffer more.

9. The strongest objection to co-education is from the moral point of view. Emotional disturbances will

take place. They are exposed to sex appeal and morals are at risk. Sex criminality will increase with co-education.

Weighing the pros and cons of the problem and considering the peculiar conditions of India, her social customs and traditions, her orthodoxy and conservativeness, it is rather difficult to introduce co-education at all stages. It can, however, be done in the primary classes where the mixing of sexes is healthy and harmless and at advanced university stage when boys and girls have developed a sense of responsibility and where it is expensive to provide separate institutions for them. At all the other stages, girls schools must be separate from boys.

Apart from these, the writer ventures to give the following suggestions:

(a) Under the prevailing social and economic conditions, there is no harm in introducing co-education.

(b) Curriculum should be prepared in such a way that it caters to the interests, needs and aptitudes of both boys and girls.

(c) Co-curricular activities, particularly N.C.C., girl guiding and physical activities should be conducted separately for girls.

(d) Equal opportunities should be offered to both boys and girls for self expression.

(e) Co-educational institutions should possess congenial climate.

(f) Teaching staff (mixed) should be extremely efficient.

(g) Separate retiring places and sanitary arrangements should exist for the girl students.

(*h*) Provision should be made for the teaching of subjects like Music, House-hold Accounts, Domestic Arithmetic, Home craft and other subjects intended for girls.

Co-Education at the Various Stages of Education

Co-education at all stages of education exists only in a few western countries like U.S.A. and U.S S.R. In others, it exists at the primary and university stages. Let us discuss its possibility at all levels.

1. Primary Stage. There are strong financial and educational reasons in favour of co-education at primary stage. At this there is absolutely no harm in having co-education especially in those areas where the number of boys and girls attending a school is too less. It becomes, rather necessary to have co-education. Separate boys and girls schools would be too expensive. It will not give rise to problems at all. The sex consciousness is absolutely dormant at this age. They are too innocent. Even from the point of view of curriculum also there is little need for differentiation. From organisational point of view, it is possible to reproduce the spirit, conditions and relations of home. At this stage, the psychological differences are not at all prominent. So no problems can possibly arise so as to pose danger.

Staff for the Primary Stage. It need not be stressed that the youngsters can be best handled by women. Since the mother is an important factor in the life of a child, a woman teacher as "mother substitute" has great potentialities. The writer has seen this system working well even in boys' schools where the primary school children are taught by female teachers. Women teachers have manners, sweet temper and dutiful nature. They are less harsh. The children love them as they love their mothers. Since women know proper handling of young ones, they are most competent to look after their educational needs. In co-educational primary schools

schools, lady teachers are a necessity. They are better fitted to do the job.

2. Secondary Stage. Co-education at this stage presents many difficulties. Boys and girls reach the adolescence stage and it is fraught with many dangers. The objections to co-education at this stage can be discussed under psychological, physiological and moral heads.

(a) **Psychological.** The emotional and temperamental differences, are noticeable at this stage. Girls attach greater importance to feelings; and sentiments, and are more serious and hard working than boys. They have a greater sense of responsibility. The interests of boys and; girls are quite different and the two cannot be taught with the same methods of teaching. Co-education at this stage will lead to premature sex stimulation which is not conducive to normal growth.

(b) **Moral.** People oppose co-education from the moral point of view. Boys and girls are extremely susceptible to sex appeal and the morals are exposed to risks. People consider co-education a monstrously immoral institution, which will result in gross corruption and criminal sexual laxity, wrecking the students completely. This is, of course, an extreme view.

Let us consider the views of the supporters of co-education with regard to morals. The co-educationists argue that wisdom lies in meeting the special dangers of the age when they arise and in directing the impulses and energies into healthy and useful channels. To run away from the problems of education is to adopt an escapist attitude. We must come to grips with the problems that arise out of it. Sex consciousness is reduced by the constant social contact of sexes. The sex relations become unsentimental with no mystery about sex. There are fewer changes of sex strains, perversions and abnormalilies. Co-education trains boys and girls for participating in the civic life on equal terms. To accept all this as correct would amount to shutting the eyes to stark realities of co-education. Some complicated problems will crop up, but they can be faced.

(c) **Physiological.** Vast physiological changes start taking place amongst boys and girls. One of the most important changes is the development of sex characteristics. There are primary sex characteristics and secondary sex characteristics. Primary sex characteristics include the development of reproductive organs while secondary sex characteristics include the development of pubic hair, appearance of beard, width of hips, development of breast etc. These changes lead to fear, and restlessness. Both find it difficult to adjust to new bodily changes and take to day-dreaming and remain pre-occupied with sex.

3. University Stage. Co-education is very much favoured at the University stage. The reasons are obvious. The students are comparatively mature and they can think of their future. By this age, they have sufficiently gained proper understanding of each other. They have also learnt to respect each other. Some of the misunderstandings about the opposite sexes, too, are properly removed. By this stage, boys and girls are supposed to have secured control over their sex impulses and to have acquired enough intelligence and discretion. The ideas and attitudes of boys and girls towards life also start taking a definite shape.

❑

10

Vocational Education in India

Indian Education Commission (1964-66) observed, "We visualize the future trend of school education to be towards a fruitful mingling of general and vocational education-general education contacting some elements of pre-vocational and technical education, and vocational education in its turn having an element of general education. In the kind of society in which we will be living in the coming years, a complete separation between the two will not only be undesirable but impossible. Vocationalisation of education at secondary stage implies Vocational training in the specific vocation so as to train the practical aptitudes of students in the preparation for definite work in future life and General education courses. Thus vocationalisation means to provide a strong vocational bias to secondary education. Vocational courses should be introduced in secondary schools alongwith general subjects. General and vocational education should not be separated.

Importance of Vocational Education

1. Solution of Economic Problems. India is today facing such grave problems as employment, poverty, famine etc. Our economic problems are our greatest difficulties. Hence, vocationalisation of education is of the greatest importance since only such education can help to solve the economic problems of our country. Mahatma Gandhi flghtly stated,

"True education ought to be for children a kind of insurance against unemployment."

2. Attainment of Happiness. The true object of education is the generation of happiness. Happiness is said to be the summum bonum of life and existence. Man is really very happy when he is adjusted to his occupation. A happy and contented individual can render best service to society. Vocationalisation of education will balance the distinctive capacity of the individual with social service.

3. Attainment of Social Efficiency. Vocationalisation of education will help the education to attain economic independence and social efficiency. Social efficiency is the outcome of the efforts of the individuals who earn their livelihood and who are not a drag on the members of the society.

4. Minimising Social Misfits. Vocationalisation of education will facilitate fixing the right person at the right place and thus minimises social misfits, entailing wastage of human talent, initiative and resourcefullness. For children of lower intelligence vocational education is the only hope. Such children should have vocational training as early as possible because they are at a great disadvantage when taught academic subjects with more intelligent children.

5. Giving Purpose to Educational Activity. Vocationalised education will be purposeful and conducive to learning. It makes the child an active partner in the learning process. It makes use of the child's tendencies and habits, pays attention to their interests and awakens their minds. It excites the intelligence and puts an end to lethargy and inactivity.

6. Moral, Intellectual and Cultural Development. As far as the vocational aspect of education is concerned, it is connected with earning money. For this reason, one expects a high moral, intellectual and cultural level from an educated individual. If the educated individual fails to win economic independence, he tends to be immoral in his behaviour; degenerates in his intellect and indifferent to the arts and cultural tastes.

Causes of Slow Progress of Vocational (Technical) Education according to Secondary Education Commission (1952-53)

1. Lack of Seriousness. The position of vocational education has not been seriously tackled comprehensively by the Central and State Governments.

2. Lack of Expert Guidance. The Department of Public Instruction in almost all states had no advantage of expert guidance to plan vocational courses on an intelligent and comprehensive basis.

3. Lack of Training Facilities. There has been a lack of training facilities for teachers for vocational courses. The teachers were not available who combined in themselves general knowledge of a sufficiently high standard and the technical and applied scientific knowledge in the branch of vocational studies.

4. Lack of Finances. There has been lack of finances to equip schools adequately and get properly trained teachers. Absence of well trained teachers and proper material facilities hindered the progress of vocational education.

5. Lack or Co-ordination. There has not been sufficient co-ordination and co-operation between the different departments of government. Some institutions were under the Director of Industries, others were under the Director of Labour and the rest under the Director of Education.

Recommendations of Secondary Education on Vocationalisation of Education

1. Diversification of Courses. Our Secondary Schools should offer a diversity of educational programmes to meet varying interests, aptitudes and talents. They should provide more comprehensive courses including general and vocational subjects and pupils should have an opportunity to choose from them according to their needs. It should be realized that if special practical subjects are taught side-by-side with certain common core subjects of general value and utility they can contribute to the all-round education of students, making them productive, co-operative, well balanced and useful members of the society.

2. Multilateral Schools. Multipurpose or multilateral schools should be started to provide diversified courses. The main advantages of multilateral schools are:

(i) ***To Remove Individuals Distinctions.*** It ramoves all individual distinctions between students preparing for different courses of studies, breaking down the sense of inferiority that is associated with vocational subject and makes it possible to plan the educational system on a truly democratic basis.

(ii) ***To Facilitate Educational Guidance.*** It provides a greater variety of educational media and thereby facilitates proper educational guidance in the choice of studies.

(iii) ***To Solve the Problem of Wrongly Classified Pupil.*** It helps to solve the problem of worngly classified pupil, because transfer within the same school is easier to arrange than transfer from one school to another.

3. Agricultural Education in Secondary Schools. Agriculture plays an important role in the national economy. In view of its basic importance, the Commission recommends that all states should provide greater opportunities for agricultural education in rural areas. Instructions in agriculture should not be theoretical only but students should be given an opportunity to work in realistic conditions.

With agriculture, two other allied subjects—Horticulture and Animal Husbandry should be closely integrated. There should be adequate plots for cultivation and agriculture should be taught scientifically. Suitable types of cottage industries should also be taught in agricultural schools. The particular type of industry chosen for a school should depend upon its location, the facilities available and the requirements of the region. It may be spinning and weaving, or leather work or pottery or basketary or arpentry or some other useful craft. It is further recommended that agricultural schools should form a part of rural multipurpose schools.

4. Technical Education. Technical education should be imparted. Secondary Commission made following recommendations concerning technical education:

- *(i) Technical Schools.* Technical schools should be started in large numbers either separately or as part of Multipurpose schools. They should provide technical as well as general education.
- *(ii) Location of Technical Schools.* Wherever possible. Technical schools should be located in close proximity to appropriate industries and they should function in close co-operation with the industry concerned.
- *(iii) Central Technical Institutes.* Central Technical Institutes should be established in large cities which may cater to the needs of several local schools.
- *(iv) Legislation for Practical Training.* Suitable legislation should be passed making it obligatory for the industry to afford facilities to students for practical training.
- *(v) Close Association.* In the planning of the technical and technological education at all levels, representatives of Commerce and industry should be closely associated with the educationists so that

in the planning and direction of such education and in the maintenance of standards their views may be given effective weight.

(vi) ***Industrial Education Cess.*** A small cess to be called "Industrial Education Cess" should be levied on industries and the proceeds of the cess should be used for the furtherance of technical education.

Multipurpose schools were started at many places but they failed to divert the students into different walks of life.

Recommendations of Kothari Commission

Kothari Commission made the following recommendations for implementing vocationalisation of education:

(1) Lower Secondary Stage. The following courses can be organized for students who leave school at the end of class VII or VIII:

1. ***Reducing the Age of Admission.*** In the Industrial Training Institutes, there are courses which are open to those who have completed the primary school. If the age of admission to these courses is reduced to 14 (this was originally 16 and now reduced to 15), a large number of students who have completed the primary school will be able to enter these courses of industrial training.

2. ***Wide Range Part-time Courses.*** A wide range of courses should be available on a part-time basis for a large number of students who drop out after class VII or VIII to enter employment in family business, some with the idea of setting up their own small-scale industry or trade. The Education Department should set up special section to help such persons to obtain suitable opportunities for training either on a

full-time or on a part-time basis and also provide them, side by side, with some general education.

3. ***Terminal Courses in Technical Schools.*** Technical high schools and junior technical schools should prepare students for jobs in industry. The courses offered should be clearly terminal and adjusted through the greater use of available time to meet the requirements of the Apprenticeship Act and should lead to trade certificates. The length of courses may vary from course to course with a strong emphasis on experimental work and applied science in all the schools.

4. ***Home-science for Girls.*** A large proportion of girls will leave school and get married either immediately or little later. They should be given further education in home science combined with general education.

5. ***To Improve Professional Efficiency and General Education.*** A large proportion of rural boys will join the family farm. They will have to be provided with further education which will enable them to improve their professional efficiency and general education.

(2) Higher Secondary Stage. At this stage Kothari Commission has recommended the following types of vocational courses:

1. ***Full-time and Part-time Vocational Courses in Industry.*** Facilities for full-time studies in agricultural and engineering polytechnics should be expanded and part-time vocational courses in industry be arranged on either a day-basis, or correspondence course basis.

2. ***Expansion of Courses in Industrial Training Institutes.*** A large number of courses offered in

Industrial Training Institutes require the completion of class X as a qualification for entry. These should be expanded rapid.

3. ***Short Condensed Courses.*** Agricultural and engineering polytechnics should organize short condensed courses for the upgrading of skills of those who have entered into employment or the re-training and re-education of those already quailed.

4. ***Developing a Wide Range of Other Courses.*** In addition to the courses so far described, a wide range of other courses in health, Commerce, administration, small-scale industries and the services should be developed ranging in duration from six months to three years for a certificate or a diploma qualification. These can be offered on a part-time basis or through correspondence for those already in employment.

5. ***Special Section for Organization of Courses.*** The State Departments of Education should create special section for the overall organisation of courses of this nature whether full-time or part-time. In organizing such programmes the manpower needs should be taken into consideration and there should be close collaboration with the machinery for vocational guidance and with industry and employers generally.

6. ***Central Grants.*** The Commission attaches great importance to the vocationalisation of secondary education. For this purpose the Commission recommends that the Central Government should provide special grants to State government in the centrally sponsored sector for programmes of vocationalisation for secondary education.

(3) Part-time Vocational Education. Another important aspect of the expansion of secondary education is the need to provide part-time education. It will have to be expanded on the following lines:

1. ***Lower Secondary Stage.*** The Commission recommends that part-time courses should be organised for those students who have completed the primary school and are unable to continue their studies on a full-time basis they wish to prepare themselves for high school examination at the end of class X. Part-time education should largely be of vocational character it is required by those who have actually adopted some career and desire to improve their professional efficiency.

2. ***Higher Secondary Stage.*** Programmes of part-time education at this stage are very important and will include the following:

    (i) Part-time course in agriculture for those who have taken to agriculture as a career.

    (ii) Special courses for girls on the lines of those recommended at the lower secondary stage, but conducted at a higher level in view of the better general education which the students would have received.

    (iii) Part-time course organised on the pattern of full-time ones meant for those who would like to pass the Higher Secondary examination.

    (iv) Part-time courses in industry for those who have joined it.

    (v) Part-time courses for those who want to be self-employed.

The Commission observes that part-time education is needed more for girls than for boys, as girls are more useful at home and they tend to be withdrawn from schools earlier than boys. The same is true of vocational education. A vast majority of girls that leave school at fourteen would be benefitted by short vocational courses or by courses in home science which would help them in their future life. These courses need greater emphasis than a mere continuation of general education.

Work-Experiences

One of the greatest weaknesses of our education is the lack of emphasis on work-experience. In the twentieth century to neglect this area of study is to deny the student an opportunity to acquaint himself with knowledge and skill which will be of vital concern to him all of his life. Work-oriented education is useful for the student throughout his life. It is necessary to build two-way bridges between education and productivity in all levels. It contributes in its own distinct way to the all round and well balanced development of an individual, as a member of the human society.

Historical Perspective. Although Hunter Commission (1882), Hartog Committee (1929) and Sapru Committee (1934), Abbot and Wood Report (1936) and Sargent Report (1944) emphasised the need of instruction in arts, crafts, technical and vocational pursuits, yet no adequate provision was made for instruction in these pursuits.

Mahatma Gandhi's idea of self supporting educational system at primary level for the village, the basic social unit of India, developed into the first indigenous efforts known as the 'Basic System of Education.' But several complex controversial issues and handicaps were involved.

Mudaliar Commission (1952-53) recommended diversified course in secondary schools. The Commission recommended Multipurpose schools. But multipurpose scheme was slowly abandoned due to variously causes like heterogeneity of the educational systems in various States, total absence or unharmonised and out of phase operational plans non-availability of proper and adequate teachers, the unchanged overall educational pattern.

Kothari Commission (1964-66) recommended work-experience as an integral part of education. While separate vocational schools have been envisaged by the Commission, it has emphasised in clear cut terms that one of the means of achieving the national goals is by linking education to productivity and this link can be forged by introducing work-experience as an integral part of general education.

Kothari Commission defines work-experience as participation in productive work in schools, in home, in a workshop, in a farm, in a factory or in another productive situation. It is clear that the productive work should be under conditions approximating to those found in real life situations.

Characteristics of Work-Experience

1. Productivity. Work-experience is related to productivity. It involves participation in productive work.

2. Wide Range of Activities. Very wide range of possible activities, can be provided in a programme of work-experience. The choice of the activity is to be determined mainly by the availability of materials, and trained instructors.

3. Work-experience at Different Stages. Work-experience should be introduced as an integral part of all education—general or vocational. In the lower classes of a primary school, work-experience may begin is simple hand-work. In the senior classes it may take the form of earning a craft. Work experience at the lower secondary stage can take the form of workshop training. At the higher secondary stage, work experience should be made available in school workshops and also on farms and industrial or commercial establishments.

4. Related to Basic Education. The concept of work-experience is closely related to the philosophy underlying basic education. What is now needed is a reorientation of basic education programme to the needs of a society that has to be transformed with the help of science and technology. In other words work-experience must be forward-looking in keeping with the character of the new social order.

5. Productive Work-experience in Rural Schools. While it is true that work-experience in rural areas could be largely built round agriculture, programmes oriented to industry and simple technology should be introduced in a fair proportion of rural schools. In such schools where school workshops cannot two provided, suitable kits of tools and materials may be manufactured at low cost and made available to the pupils.

6. Increasing Facilities. It should be declared objective of State policy to increase the facilities for work-experience in industry and agriculture as rapidly as possible and to make them available to schools for the education of the rising generation. A continuous attempt should be made to bring in science and technology and to introduce the pupils to better ways of performing the traditional productive tasks.

Need and Importance of Work-Experience

Modern educationists unanimously agree that work-experience should be introduced as an integral part of education at all stages in schools. Work-experience is useful from the following points of view:

1. ***Corrective to Bookish Education.*** Work-experience provides corrective to the over academic bookish nature of our education. It shifts the existing emphasis on book-learning to relating knowledge actively to socially oriented productive work. It removes the boredom of unrelieved academic work and the consequent mental strain by using the psychological

principle of alteration between mental, manual and physical activities in order to give suitable rest spans to the brain-cells and muscles.

2. ***Acquaintance With Modern Technology.*** Work-experience acquaints the students with the tools, processes and materials of modern technology. The students can acquire knowledge about the sources from where raw materials can be obtained, their specifications, their method of identification, processes of their manufacture and the physical, chemical and mechanical properties etc. The students can learn the method of selection, the use and maintenance of apparatus and tools used in the production activities in which they are engaged.

3. ***Productive Competency.*** Work experience develops productive competency to earn some amount. A successful programme of work-experience should make the student participate in some type of work in real life and may ultimately develop in him enough productive competency to earn some money.

4. ***Dignity of Labour.*** Work experience inculcates in the students sense of dignity of labour, self-reliance and spirit of enterprise and habit of hard work. These students can learn to undertake hard and constant physical work, as manual labour is one of the most important elements of a work-experience programme.

5. ***Insight and Forward Look.*** Work-experience provide insight and forward look to the students in improving the tools and techniques of production, doing every work methodically and avoiding every kind of wastage. Through the dynamic and forward looking nature of work experience a new society can develop with deeper interest in work.

6. ***Solution to Problems of Daily Life.*** Work-experience helps in solving problems of daily life of the students of their family and their community. For ordinary repair of our belongings—electric appliances, stove, watch, bicycle etc. we are required to run to the market and spend lot of money. A student who has work-experience will be more successful in his practical life than otherwise. Work-experience enables the individual to live as a self-sufficient and healthy individual.

7. ***Recreation.*** Work-experience provides recreation. It provides necessary setting for holding recreational and cultural activities. For example, holding of exhibitions and activities like to making and making of scientific instruments provide lot of joy and entertainment to students.

8. ***Good Work Habits.*** Work experience inculcates good work habits and desirable traits of character. It motivates students to live in co-operation with others. The students can learn safety precautions to be observed during production activities. The students can learn the procedure of selection and proper use of consumer goods.

9. ***Educational and Vocational Guidance.*** Work experience provides educational and vocational guidance. A successful work-experience programme provides useful activities so that students energies and enthusiasm are properly channelized. With the help of a work-experience programme a guidance teacher can help students to offer educational and vocational courses.

10. ***Solution to Problem of Indiscipline.*** Work-experience solves the problem of indiscipline The surplus zeal

and energy of students can be utilised in work experience programmes. Once their interest in the work is aroused they will not find time for activities involving indiscipline. Experience base shown that even brightest students take great interest in work-experience activities.

The development of work-oriented education is in the national interest because it is essential to the national economy, defence and welfare. It develops consciousness to avoid wastage of every kind.

Kothari Commission on Programmes of Work-Experience

1. Work-Experience in the Lower Primary Classes (I to IV or V).

Simple Hand-Work. In the lower classes of the primary school work-experience may begin as simple hand-work. The activities, suggested are: paper cutting, card-board work, clay modelling, spinning, simple needle work, simple planting indoors or on plots and kitchen gardening.

The objective of introducing work-experience at this stage is to train children to make use of their hands and thereby help their intellectual growth.

2. Work-Experience in the Higher Primary Classes (IV/V to VII/VIII)

Learning of Craft. In the higher primary classes, work-experience may take the form of learning a craft which develops technical thinking and creative capacities in the pupils. The crafts recommended are: cane and bamboo work, leather work, pottery, needle-work, weaving gardening, model making, fret-work and work on farms.

3. *Work-Experience in the Lower Secondary Stage (Classes VII/VIII to X)*

Workshop Training. At this stage work-experience should be productive. It should be provided in real life situations. The activities recommended at this stage are: wood work, simple metal work, basket work, leather work, ceramics, soap making, tanning, preserving, weaving, electrical repairs, cookery, model making, making simple scientific equipment, class-room decoration, carpet making, book-binding, fabric printing, tailoring, toy making, millinery, wood carving, simple farm mechanics, animal care, crop care, care of the soil and workshop practice.

It is suggested by the Commission that at the lower secondary stage work-experience should take the form of workshop training. Accordingly it has been suggested that a workshop should be attached to every school or a group of secondary schools in a phased manner over the next ten years (by 1976).

4. *Work-Experience in Higher Secondary Classes (XI-XII)*

Work Experience in Farms, Commercial or Industrial Concerns. Many of the activities listed, at the lower secondary stage should be continued at this stage but emphasis should shift to workshop practice of actual work experience in industrial or commercial concern sort on farms. The activities should be oriented towards productive work. Skills demanded in wood work, metal work and agriculture should be of a higher and more exacting nature.

Thus we find that the range of possible activities that can be provided in a programme of work-experience is very wide, and the choice should be determined merely by the availability of materials and trained instructors.

National Seminar on Primary and Work- Oriented Education (1970)

1. Need to Spell Out the Details. The seminar emphasised the need to spell out the details pertaining to the following aspects of work experience:

(i) Formulation of the operational concept of work-experience.

(ii) Types of work-experience programmes to be introduced during 1970's in the country.

(iii) Minimum work-experience programmes to be introduced in schools in the country with stress on the structured activities to be introduced in selected schools.

(iv) Action programmes pertaining to production of curriculum materials.

(v) The pre-service and in-service training geared to work-experience to be provided to teachers and supervisors.

(vi) Steps to be taken for mobilisation of public opinion in favour of work experience.

2. Socially Useful Work-Experience. The seminar endorsed the view that work-experience should be socially meaningful, realistic, physical work—without over emphasis on economic aspects at the cost of learning outcomes.

3. Encouragement to Individual Schools. The seminar pointed out that individual schools might be encouraged to develop their own programmes of work-experience.

4. Need of Developing Minimum Work-Experience Programme. The seminar stressed the need to develop a minimum work-experience programme suitable to each state.

Problems in Implementing the Programme of Work-Experience

Kothari Commission observed that in implementing the programme of work-experience, three problems have to be tackled:

1. ***Problem of Training of Teachers.*** There is a problem of non-availability of right type of teachers for work-experience. The following solutions are suggested:

    (i) *Work-experience as a Subject in Teacher-training Institutions.* Work-experience should be introduced as a compulsory subject in teacher-training institutes at all levels and effective training in work-experience should be provided. Since there are already some facilities for the teaching of craft in a large number of training institutions, it would be worthwhile to improve the teaching of craft.

    (ii) *Short Term and in-service Training Course.* Arrangements should be made for short-term and in-service training courses for teachers.

    (iii) *Recruitting Skilled Craftsmen.* Teachers at the lower secondary stage should be recruited from skilled craftsmen trained by the Industrial Training Institutes diploma holders in agriculture etc. The Regional Colleges of Education of NCERT have also started courses for teachers of industrial arts. Such a teacher might work in one school or be used as part-time teachers for a group of schools.

    Craftsmen or persons engaged in factories or forms conversant with modern modes of production can also serve as a useful purpose. It will be desirable to seek the co-operation of the teachers in Polytechnics or Industrial Training Institutes to work as part-time teachers.

(iv) *Two-year Art and Craft Teachers Course.* At the higher primary stage it is suggested by the Commission that State Government should review the position regarding training of craft teachers in their States. It is good idea to have a combined two-year art and craft teachers course for teachers working at this stage.

2. ***Problem of Facilities and Equipment.*** There is problem of facilities and equipment. To solve this problem the following suggestions are given:

(i) *Utilising Private Farms.* Where it is not possible to attach farms to school, arrangements should be made to obtain the assistance of local people to provide work-experience to the student on private farms.

(ii) *Attaching Farms to Schools.* In rural areas, farms should be attached to schools wherever possible.

(iii) *Co-operation of Industrial Concerns.* The help of industrial concerns should be enlisted to design and manufacture cheap kits for schools and materials which can be used by groups of children and graded for the different school levels. Standardised design of tools and simple equipment needs might also be given to Industrial Training Institutes, Polytechnics, vocational schools and conceivably engineering colleges for manufacture as part of their training programmes.

(iv) *Facilities for Industry-oriented Experience.* Facilities for industry-oriented experience should be

provided in all the bigger schools. All secondary schools, whether urban or rural, should be provided with workshops

3. ***Problem of Development of the Programme.*** There is a problem of development of the programme. The following suggestions are offered in this direction:

   (i) *Preparation of Necessary Literature.* Necessary literature about the scheme should be prepared and introduced to teachers and schools.

   (ii) *Training of Special Teachers.* The training of special teachers needed for the programme should be undertaken in advance.

   (iii) *Orientation Courses for Officers.* Short orientation courses should be held for officers of the department, principals and headmasters.

Many and varied programmes of work-experience have been introduced and are being implemented in several schools in various states. Various nomenclatures have also been used to characterise these programmes *viz.*, "Earn while you Learn Scheme," "Air Vice Marshall Scheme", "Occupation-oriented Programme", "The Job and Hobby-oriented Programme" etc. Preparatory work in this connection has been undertaken by Punjab Government in 1974-75, and 100 middle and 50 higher secondary schools have been chosen for inclusion in the programme in 1975-76.

It has been observed during the implementation of some programmes that:

1. They are being offered only to those who are interested and not for all students.

2. They sometimes reduce themselves to the traditional craft work; (3 times a week, one period each).

3. They virtually become just social service deeds.
4. They emphasise the monetary return aspect to the total detriment of others.
5. They are simultaneously introduced for all classes in school, say for classes 5 to 10, and that too in one area.

It should be noted that experiencing representative samples of production processes has not been completely understood and appreciated by workers in the field. Improvement in implementing work-experience programme is needed. An additional task would be the introduction of the programmes in these institutions and classes where they are not operating at present. But flexible approach should be followed in the implementation of work-experience and maximum freedom should be given to each school to select its own activities in accordance with the needs of the local community.

❑

11

Computer and Internet Education

Progress in the field of science and technology has worked wonders in the different walks of life. The latest advancement is of computers and their successive use for instructional purposes. In the developed countries like U.S.S.R., U.S.A., Canada etc. computer facility has reached every educational institution. But in our country, its need and importance has been recognised increasingly and efforts are afoot to have it and make use of it in different facets of life. Only in limited institutions, computers are being used for the instructional purposes. Computer can work wonders almost in every field of human activity. Countless number of calculations within a second are possible with the help of a computer.

A computer is a power-driven machine equipped with keyboards, electronic circuit, storage compartments and recording devices for the high speed performance of mathematical operations. It has also a capacity for storing of memorising a large amount of information and producing any of them when called for. We may say that the computer is a box loaded with information. It has its own symbolical language. In order to work on a computer or to derive benefit, we shall have to familiarise ourselves with the language of the computer. So we shall have to feed the computer first. Then it interacts and manipulates the information, translates the answer and types it on a tele-type-writer.

Important Parts of a Computer

There are five important parts of a computer which are briefly explained below:

1. The input equipment of the computer is in the form of key board and cassette recorder. It receives the outside information so that it may work accordingly.
2. The memory part contains all information which has been fed into the computer. It helps in storing information and retaining it. Further it can be used whenever needed.
3. The output equipment translates information back into understandable form.
4. The processing unit is the arithmatic and logic mind of the computer which is responsible for all types of date manipulation and computation work.
5. The control sub-system controls the execution of the programme and co-ordinate all the activities of the sub-system of the computer.

The computer is a hardware machine. The software used in it is in the form of written programme which is prepared by the computer programme writer. The computer works as the programmer directs it. The computer in itself is not an independent thinking machine.

Computers have their own languages. They are known by different technical names Basic, Logo, Pilot, Cobol etc. We should understand the languages of the computers if we want to communicate with them. Most of the computers make use of binary system, where two digits symbol 0 and 1 are used for expressing any number.

For Example,

Step I. Number	**Computer Language**
0	0000
1	0001
2	0010
3	0011
4	0100
5	0101
6	0110
7	0111
8	1000

Step II. Then the operations are given code numbers as given below :

Operations	**Code Number**
Add	1
Subract	2
Multiply	3
Divide	4
Read a card	5
Square	6
Draw a line	7
Transform	8

Step III. At this stage, the code numbers are transformed in computer language as suggested above in step I.

According to J. Bruchner, there are two systems for computerized instruction:

1. In computer assisted instruction, the student participates with the computer system on a direct basis and the instructional materials are stored in the computer system.

2. Computer managed instructions are used to help the teacher to administer and guide the instructional process but relies on separate hardware and learning materials; the student is usually not on line with the computer system and the processing need not be in real time. Instructional materials are not stored in the computer system.

Advantages of Computer

We can use the computer as an effective and indispensable aid in the teaching-learning process. Below are given a few advantages:

1. It helps the learners in the development of variety of skills. It can also be used for providing drill and practice to the learners.

2. The computer can play efectively the role of a tutor by maintaining perfect interaction and dialogue with the individual students.

3. They can be used to develop problem solving ability and creativity among the students.

4. It can serve the role of an inquiry officer. The students put questions and it gives response with the help of answers it has already stored.

5. The computers can be used to give training to the students through simulated and gaming techniques.
6. They can be used in providing education to the handicapped children like deaf and dumb.
7. They can supplement laboratory and other practical work specially in science subjects.

Drawbacks of Computer

The computer assisted instructions suffer from some drawbacks which are given below:

1. The use of computers in the classrooms is very expensive and uneconomical in terms of educational returns.
2. Handling the computer is rather technical. There is always the danger of damaging the costly machine by the students.
3. It is rather difficult to teach all subjects and all topics with the help of a computer. There is dearth of computer programmes for teaching purposes.
4. Being auto-instructional, it may lead to indiscipline, truancy, carelessness and wastage of time on the part of some students.
5. The repair work or its servicing causes a serious problem to the institutions.
6. Heavy school curriculum and shortage of trained personels pose a threat to the introduction of computer assisted instruction in the educational institution.

Role of Computer in Education

In 1965, Lorence Settlor and Daniel Davis developed most complicated teaching processes in which computer was used for presenting instructions in place of teacher. They divided the teaching process of the computer in two parts :

1. Pre-tutorial phase.
2. Tutorial phase.

In the first phase, computer assisted instruction is given to the pupils to achieve the specific objectives on the basis of his entering behaviour. In the second phase, instructing material is presented accordingly. The pupil studies it. Then, the achievement of the pupil is evaluated. After presenting the instruction, computer also controls it. It also provides reinforcement to the pupils.

In the modren age, the use of computers in the field of education, made in following areas :

(i) All the researchers do all analytical tasks with the help of computers in the research work.

(ii) Computers' help is sought for preparing the results of the examinations.

(iii) Computers are also used in educational guidance and counselling.

(iv) Remedial teaching of the pupils is also done by the computers.

Computer Programmes

While observing groups of students working with the computer, you would notice that students enthusiastically participate in the learning programme. The computer's novelty, the challenge involved in the programme, the wonderful display of tasks—all help in creating and sustaining their motivation. Learning with the computer is never full and monotonous. Some of examples are given below:

1. Codebreaker. It is a programme which keeps asking questions and the students supply the answers. In pedagogic terms this question-answer sequence provides an opportunity for useful interaction which is essential for successful learning.

2. Varietext. It is part of the text with blanks for the students to fill in. For each blank four alternatives appear one after another and the student has to choose the most appropriate one. Whenever necessary, the student can get the computer to display the correct words. This instant feed-back is apart of the progarmme and no other technological instrument can be faster than the computer in providing such instant feedback.

2. Yellow River Kingdom. It is problem-solving activity. The computer displays a vast kingdom with a lot of resources. The Computer is capable of simulating such complicated situations for the purpose of teaching learning. It can be simulated dangerous situations such as burning forest or division of atom.

Pedagogic Qualities of the Computer

1. Motives the learners.
2. Stimulates situations which are difficult and dangerous.
3. Interacts with the learners.
4. Provides instant feedback.
5. Distance Education.

Such a powerful instrument has several uses in the field of distance education where technological media are a basic necessity. There is hardly any distance education institution in the world which does not make use of media such as radio and T.V. Regular, though in a small scale, radio broadcasts and TV telecasts are a part of distance education courses in India too.

Some of the major advantages of using computers in distance education are as follows :

(i) Computer brings flexibility and individuality to the study process.

(ii) Computer stimulated students to experiment, design and create solutions to the problems.

(iii) Computer reduces the isolating of distance learners.

(iv) Computer-based study materials are cost-effective when produced on a large scale.

The increasing availability of micro-computers in the developed countries offered major new opportunities for distance education. The computer has various applications for distance learning. It can be used as a teaching medium, a learning tool, a manager of learning or as an aid to educational administration.

Applications of Computers

1. Budgeting and monitoring of finances.
2. Keeping students records.
3. Maintaining statistics.
4. Monitoring materials production register and so on.
5. Mailing of rest score.
6. Student billing.
7. Preparation of payroll, bills and debts ledger.

Instructional Situations of Computer Application

1. Pretesting of students knowledge on enrolment.
2. Planning and printing individualized programmes.

3. Monitoring students progress.
4. Compilling tests and scores etc. A number of such data files can be stored in the computer.

Other contributions of computers are word processing to aid course development and data processing to aid administration. In addition, electronic mail is also used to communicate, change and exchange materials. The course teams can also use computers for conferences, establishing a communication channel among multiple writers and other professionals.

'On-line' and 'Off-line' Computers

Computers can be used in distance learning in two modes—local mode and transmitted mode—local mode or 'off-line' computer stands on its own as an independent system helping the learner to work on his own. In transmitted mode, one computer is connected to another computer which is 'on-line' and then the operation depends upon communication between these devices. By inter-connecting the computers, a complex learning Network can be created which could link all distance learners with their teacher and with a central institution.

New technologies in Education

Information Technology broadly deals with the application of technology in the field of information. In this process, media, computer, operations related to hardware and internet play a vital role in education especially in class-room instruction. New technologies which are emerging need to be integrated in order to provide meaningful and complete information. An effort to this direction has led to constitute a NETWORK. It makes the flow of information very simple, easy, and effective on the part of transmitter (teacher) and receiver (student).

The basic structure involved in NETWORK is :

(i) Interlinkages. Different components involved in Information Technology are interconnected. The relevant information is passed on from one channel to another. The whole NETWORK is based on the nature and type of interlinkages (interconnectivity).

(ii) Communication. The second component in INTERNET is effective communication. Messages are passed on from one place to another. Information reaches from one point to another. Without any loss of information, complete message is commnunicated.

(iii) System. NETWORK operates through a system. There are sub-systems. Each sub-system performs its function. The integrated one whole of sub-systems leads to work as much expanded and multiple functions.

NETWORK is a vast cyberspace where one can gather, disseminate and exchange all types of information. An arrangement consisting of two or more computers is called NETWORK. It is a physical medium used to transport the data. A computer network is created when several computers are linked by data communication channels. Each computer in a network can have its own processing capabilities and can also share hardware, data files and programmes. Following are the types of Computer Network:

1. Local Area Network. A local area network is two or more computers directly linked with in a small well defined area such as a room, building or a group of closely placed buildings. A LAN may be made up of only microcomputers or any combination of micro-computers and large systems.

A Local Area Network usually consists of the following:

(i) Two or more computers.

(ii) Software to control the operation of the computers.

(iii) Peripheral devices such as printers and hard-disk drives.

(iv) Special cables.

(v) A plug in board to handle the data transmission.

2. MAN (Metropolitan Area Network). Man is basically a bigger version of a LAN, and normally used similar technology. It might cover a group of nearby corporate offices or a city and might be either private or public. A MAN just has one or two cables and does not contain switching elements. A MAN can support both data and voice and might even be related to the local cable television network.

3. WAN (Wide Area Network). A WAN is two or more computers that are geographically dispesed, linked by communication facilities such as telephone system or microwaves relays. This type of network is usually limited to use by large corporations and government agencies because of the high costs involved in building and manitaining them.

The main difference between a WAN and LAN is that, the LAN is under the complete control of the owner, whereas the WAN needs the involvement of another authority like telecom department.

— LANs are successful and capable of handling very high data transfer rates at low cost because of the small area covered.

— LANs have a lower error rate than WANs.

Types of WAN—

There are mainly two types of WAN :

— Public Networks.

— Private Networks.

Public Networks. Public Netowrks are those Networks which are installed and run by the telecommunication authorities and are made available to any organisation or individual who go for their subscription.

Private Networks. The basic technique used in all forms of Private WAN is to use private circuits to link the locations to be served by the network. Between these fixed points the owners of the network have complete freedom to use the circuits in any way they want.

INTERNET

Internet is a World-wide Computer Network that contains a large collection of information which could be made avaliable to you on your computer. The person having internet connection can retrieve any information of individual interest.

Internet is the abbreviation of Inter-network System. The Internet is the name for a vast, worldwide system consisting of people, information and computers. It is also described as a network of networks because these are more than one lakh readily accessible through the Internet. Internet is the largest and most complete learning tool for a group of people with varied educational backgrounds and interests. Teachers, students, businessmen and other educators can share ideas instantly across vast distances. For scientific and research community, internet is an essential and indispensable tool.

Through Internet Scientists can gain and enjoy instant access to the world's most advanced research facilities and discuss their research problems with others, working in the same field.

It also serves as an encyclopaedia since one can get the desired information in detail on any subject of his interest.

History of Internet

ARPANET (Advanced Research Projects Agency Network) laid the foundation of today's Internet almost three decades ago. It was establised to test the security of a network.

Advantages of Internet

Internet is playing a very important role in the National Development by giving the following major benefits to the citizens world-wide :

—Education
—Shopping
—Advertising
—Financial Services
—Government
—Careers and so on.

Using the Internet's vast resources, one can communicate with people from all over the world and about any desired subject of choice.

APPLICATION OF INTERNET

Internet being a network of networks spread world-wide is capable of offering the following major services :

(a) E-Mail

(b) WWW (World Wide Web)

Electronic-mail

E-mail is an application in which any user as a network can send/receive letters on his computer terminal to/from any person in the world who has an electronic mail address. Internet provides a world-wide electonic mail facility.

The gerneral format of Internet e-mail address is :

< name of addressee > @ < identity of his dept. >

< Institution > < identity of Indian Network > < country code >.

Mail can be sent only to individuals but to groups, by using group identity. The Network takes care to see that the mail is delivered safely if it leaves the user's terminal.

WWW

World-wide web offers facilities to the users to share information with others. This is the fastest growing part of the internet. The web is a vast network of documents and it also gives access to every internet service. The Web server can publish text and graphics including sound and video.

Website

Website makes a user as a node of internet. This means that if a university decides to float its own website, then all information regarding admission, scholarships, rules and regulations, courses it offers, department, staff and their profiles, workshops, conferences, seminars to be conducted etc., can be kept at university's computer centre. This computer can be accessed by any member on Internet for any particular course: it will be automatically listed with all its details. This website is important to a university or a company to offer 24 hours services and on line help to international clients.

Developing a website on Internet is a costly affair as far as hardware and other costs are concerned.

The need for counting and calculating was felt as early as the Stone Age. The primitives used pebbles to count their cattle and other food stuff. Later, with the production of surplus goods, goods started getting exchanged for rice and other similar commodities, resulting in the Barter System.

Still later, people used to count by putting tally marks on sand or stone. A need for counting became more urgent giving rise to the development of various counting systems and devices.

Abacus. The Chinese developed the Abacus, a manual calculator of sorts in as early as 3000 BC. In about 1000 BC, Greeks and Egyptians improved upon it. The final version, can still be seen being used in Hong Kong and other parts of China.

Leibnitz Machine. In 1964, Gottfried Wilheim Leibnitz improved Pascaline and called it Stepped recliner or Leibnitz machine, it could multiply and divide as well as find square roots.

Pascal's Calculating Machine. In 1642 AD, Blaise Pascal, a young French scientist, developed a mechanical calculating machine, known after his name and called Pascal's Calculating machine. This machine was capable of performing only addition and subtraction. It was also called Palestine.

Analytical Engine. In 1833 AD, Charles Babbage, invented a Difference Engine to generate logarithmic and stromatal tables of numbers upto 6 places. The technique he used was the computations of successive differences. Later he developed, the concept of Analytical Engine, a calculating machine, which still forms the base of all computers. He however, could not complete his work during his lifetime. For his fundamental research he is known as the father of computers.

His work was completed by Lady Augusta Add loveless, daughter of Lord Byron, the English poet. She developed the essential ideas of programming the analytical Engine. For her contribution she is known as the first Computer Programmer.

5. Hollerith's Machine. Herman Hallerith, an American statistician developed a punch-card machine in 1887 AD. This machine could store the results in the form of punched cards and read them later on. Hollerith formed a company called Tabulating and Calculating? Company of America. It combined with other companies to form what is now known as IBM (International Business Machines Corporation, USA). IBM is among the largest manufacturers of computers in the world.

6. Mark I. In collaboration with IBM Howard Aiken of Harvard University developed 'Automatic Sequence Controlled Calculator' or Mark I. This was the first commercial computer available in the market. IBM marketed it in 1944. It was the fastest electro-mechanical machine, capable of multiplying in 4 seconds and dividing in 10 seconds. It was a huge structure, 15 meters long, 2.5 meters high and weighing 31 tons, having around 750,000 parts. At the same time came into existence the use of electronics in computers. Computers like ENIAC, EDVAC, and UNIVAC were developed. These were all huge and very expensive machines mainly used for research and development work.

7. Three Generation Computers. The principle of On Switch and Off Switch, that is the two states represented by 1 and 0, was used here. First, electronic devices, vacuum tubes were used to provide On and Off conditions. This formed the 1st Generation of Computers (1940-52). Then transistors replaced vacuum tubes forming 2nd Generation (1952-64) reducing overall size of components required for the computers. Next were Integrated Circuits or ICs also called the Chips. These were made of a material called silicon. A small silicon chip had hundreds of transistors forming ON (1) or Off (0) conditions in a very small space. This was third generation computers (1965-71).

8. Around 1972 to Till Data. Several more transistors and other electrical components like capacitors were added on to this IC to make large scale integration (LSI). In fact, a chip had an entire CPU on it and was called a micro processor resulting in smaller size, faster speed and lower cost of operations. Our present day ICs belong to 4th Generation.

Research is going on for increasing the speed of operations, decreasing the size and adding more components on a chip to give human like intelligence to computers.

Kinds of Computers

1. IBM 650. In 1955, this was launched by IBM. It was one of those big computer requiring full room to store with cables running underground to connect the various components of the machine.

This machine actually madethe scientist sit back and think of crating new machines, which could work faster and would take less space.

2. Apple PC. In 1977, this computer was developed by two young men in their twenties, named Steve Worzniak and Steve Jobbs. It became very popular for home and small business use. They formed, Apple Computers the company which manufactured more small computers than any other computer manufacturer of the time. Over the years the company has grown tremendously and has Macintosh brand of computers available throughout the world. Their computers are better than those manufactured by IBM.

3. Personal Computers (PCs). In 1981, the IBM launched its first Personal Computer called IBM-PC, since then, manufacturers other than IBM have also developed PCs which are of the same standard as that of the IBM. While IBM-PC remains the trademark of IBM, the other manufacturers market their small computers as PCs, which are also called IBM-PC compatible machines. PC has become a general term including all kinds of personal computers from IBM and other companies. PC has been improved over the years as per the following development stages:

(i) PC-I. A PC with a single floppy diskette drive. This PC had a 51/4" double sided diskette can could store upto 360 kilobytes of data. It was based on Intel 8088 IC chip. The computer operated at 4.77 Megahertz speed and had a memory of 640KB.

(ii) PC-II. A sort of extension of the PC-I computer mentioned above. Instead of single floppy drive, it had two of them. Rest of the features remained the same.

(iii) PC-XT. Developed in 1982, Personal Computer with extended Technology, had an additional fixed hard disk drive and a floppy disk drive. The microprocessor used was Intel 8088; however, the speed was increased to 8 megahertz. The usual capacity of hard disk was 20 Megabytes.

(iv) PC-AT. Developed in 1984, Personal Computer with Advanced Technology, also had a floppy drive and a hard disk drive in a minimum configuration. It could also have, within the system box, a maximum of 2 floppy drives and 2 hard disk drives. The floppy diskette used were of Double sided High Density and could store data upto 1.2 Megabytes. The capacity of a hard disk also increased from 20 to 80 Megabytes and been beyond that. The speed was also increased to 13Mhz (Megahertz) because of use of new Intel 80286 chip. The memory also increased from 640KB to standard of 1 MB but could be increased to 16 MB.

(v) PC-AT/386, 586. From 1985, through 1997, and beyond, advancements in computer technology has brought about Intel processor chips in market ranging from 80386 to 80585 in such a short span of time. Now a days 80586 chip which is also known as Pinetum is used in the computer system.

AT/386 introduced 1.44MB mini floppy of 3½", which revolutionized floppy system to such an extent that the new computers now do not have 5¼" floppy drives.

Hard disk capacity also went on increasing from 80MB to 1.2GB, in between experimenting with 256MB, 512MB and

800MB etc. Even 1.2 GB is now replaced with 2.1 GB and even 4.3 GB are available presently.

The memory chip which was IBM in case of XT, increased to 4MB, 8MB, 16MB, 32MB and even higher.

Speed of processing also kept on increasing. It was 4.77 Mhz in case of XT and then went on to 50Mhz and then on to 133Mhz and now 200MHz is the standard. PCz with speeds of 400MHz are also available.

(vi) Pentium PC. The optimum machine these days, it has a hard disk of 2.1 GB. The memory is of 32MB. It has one floppy drive of 3½", 1.44MB capacity. The clock speed is 200MHz and is based on latest Intel chip called Pentium.

(vii) Pentium MMX. The new version of Pentium chip which supports the multimedia operations like audio speakers, video card capabilities and has all these features built-in on to the single chip of the system is called Motherboard.

(vii) Pentium II-Processor. A new, more powerful processor has been developed by Intel Corporation. In its competition, Cyirx Corporation, US has produced equivalent micro-processors. K-6 and K-7.

Another American Company—Motrolla has developed another series of micro-processors-68000 series, which are mainly used in the Apple-Macintosh computers.

(ix) Power PC. There is also consortium of Apple. IBM and Motrolla which manufactures Power PC. Power P/C is supposed to take advantage of all the features of the IBM-PC compatible machines (PCs) and the MacIntosh (ac) machines. Programmes written both or the PC and the Macwill run on the Power PC machines.

❐

12

Teacher Education

A great change was needed after independence because of the changed social and political conditions. The traditional system of education with its attendant defects did not suit the new conditions. Along with the change in the educational pattern teacher's training had to be considered afresh. It is now being based and conducted according to the needs of the pupils and also of the society.

After Independence many types of teacher's training courses were started throughout the country. While in the Punjab there have been two types of teacher-education courses, one Junior Basic Training (now two years duration) meant for elementary school teachers and the other B.T., B.Ed., (one years's duration) for secondary school teachers. At present in Punjab, there is B.Ed. course for secondary school teachers. B.T. has been abolished from 1966. In fact B.T. has merged into B.Ed., and there is a change in the syllabus.

In other states even three years courses have been started for elementary school teachers. There is also M.Ed. of one year after B.T. or B.Ed. in all the provinces. In some universities research in education is being done by post graduates at the Ph.D. stage.

In-service Education Programme. In-service education programme is undertaken these days to enable the teacher to grow professionally. The holding of short-term courses, workshops, seminars and conferences for teachers in service is the responsibility of the State Education Departments. The Ministry of Education, Government of India has set up a Department of Extension services in a number of training colleges with the financial assistance from the Ford Foundation. The Extension Services Department performs the following activities :

1. Holding of workshops, seminars, group work and conferences.
2. Arranging educational exhibitions.
3. Guidance programme.
4. Audio-visual aids service.
5. Publication of literature.
6. Short and long term courses.

Importance of Training of Teachers

The importance of teachers in the educational programme of a country is too great. They are the pivot of the system. It is the teachers who interpret the curriculum and aids of instruction. It is they who give an impress of their personality to the children. The teachers have played an important role in the making of a nation. The quality of men in a country are determined by the type of teachers that a country possesses. Teachers work as active agents in ushering forth a new social order and economic policies which in turn affect educational policies.

Need for Training

Seventy percent of the teachers are trained and the rest are untrained. The percentage of trained women teachers is too low. To cope with this ever increasing demand we need more training schools and colleges because profession training is necessary. There was a belief sometimes ago that teachers are born and not made. Mastery of the subject-matter was all that was expected of a teacher. With the advancement in sciences and humanities, the old belief has changed now. Teaching now is regarded as an expert's job and as such some sort of training is deemed essential. In fact, the whole concept about teachers and teacher education has undergone a great change.

1. Education has been Psychologised. A trained teacher understands the child better. Pedagogy demands that the teacher should know the subject as well as the child. What a mighty change in education? Formerly the teacher was required to know the subject matter and not the child.

2. Education is more Than Teaching Learning. Education is not merely confined to the study of books. It has to consider other co-curricular activities for the wholesome development of the child's personality. An untrained teacher will be at a loss to undertake all these responsibilities properly.

3. Training Equips the Teacher Properly. It has been realised that there are certain qualities which a teacher acquires through training alone; these are physical, intellectual, social and emotional qualities. Professional efficiency is increased.

4. Teaching-Learning Process Needs Motivation. Before giving knowledge, the children are mentally prepared for it. They have to be active participants in the process. A trained teacher would be adept in using aids and other material for properly motivating them.

5. Training Essential for Effective Education. Training of teachers is of great importance to make education effective. Education degenerates into formal instruction in the hands of untrained teachers. Education becomes meaningless and dull under their charge. Training prepares the teacher for his job and makes him competent. He discovers his ability and makes proper use of it. Education, therefore, is rendered more effective at the hands of trained teachers.

6. Teaching is a Complex Affair. Teaching is not as simple as it used to be in the past. It has become more complex. A teacher has to be well-equipped and hence the need for training. A teacher has to look after the social adjustment and emotional integration of the child.

7. Essential for Professional Growth. For efficient and perfect teaching, professional growth of the teacher is necessary. Training prepares the teachers under training for a new calling in life and gives a purpose to it.

From the above mentioned points, it is quite obvious that teacher's training is of paramount importance if we wish to raise general standards of teaching and learning. With the diversification of courses, the teacher has to come occupy an important place in the educational system. An untrained teacher cannot fit into it.

Teacher Training Programme

The training of teachers in India can be classified under several heads. For different kinds of teachers, there are various kinds of teacher training programmes obtaining at different stages/levels.

1. Primary Training Centres. Training of teachers for pre-primary students is very important. Unfortunately facilities for pre-primary training are meagre in our country. At present there are nearly 40 training centres for primary class teachers. These different types of centres under this head—Nursery, Kindergarten, Montessori and the Pre-basic etc. The number of these institutions should be increased.

2. State Institutes of Education. These were set up in each state during the 3rd Plan Period. No regular courses are run by these institutes. These mostly provide in-service courses for teachers, teacher educators and the inspection personnel. These institutions besides organising workshops, seminars and short orientation courses also undertake the publication of literature and solving the problems of primary school teachers. These institutions serve as a guide to all those connected with primary education.

3. Training Colleges for Secondary Teachers. There are two types of secondary school teachers—graduates and under-graduates and training exists for both. For the under graduates the duration of the course is one or two years, while for the graduates it is one year. The former are awarded diplomas either by the university or education department, and the latter are given a degree by the university. There is some difference in the curriculum of these courses but basic training remains the same. Some differences may be found from one state to another. The graduates and post-graduates receive training in training-colleges whose number is about 250 in the country. These colleges are both owned by the state governments or private bodies and are mostly co-educational. Some institutions are exclusively for women.

4. Training Schools for Primary Teachers. In view of the introduction of the compulsory primary education in practically all the states and the growing consciousness among the people to send their children to schools, there has been a considerable expansion of training schools for primary teachers. The number of such institutions is in the neighbourhood of 1250. These training centres are open to men and women teachers; some are centirely for men while others exclusively for women. Only a few are co-educational. This training is open to Matric pass and the duration of the course is one to two years. It differs from state to state.

5. Regional College of Education. These institutions prepare teachers for technological subjects, agriculture, commerce and other practical streams in the various multipurpose schools. Four regional training colleges exist—one each at Ajmer, Bhopal, Bhubneshwar and Mysore. These colleges are managed by the National Council of Educational Research and Training. These provide one year courses for graduates in technology, commerce, agriculture, home science and science, an integrated four years' course for higher secondary pass candidates for similar subjects, special courses for industrial craft teachers and other short term in-service courses and programmes.

6. Post Graduate Training Courses. After the B.T. and B.Ed. Courses, facilities for post-graduate degrees also exist in colleges and universities. These are M.Ed. and Ph.D. Courses. Besides these, there are diploma courses in special areas such as Educational Administration, Guidance and Counselling.

Existing Programmes of Teacher Education

After achieving independence, there has been a good deal of expansion in training schools and colleges. With expansion, numerous problems have arisen which require our immediate attention. The standards of training have gone down. There is no planned working of training institutions in the country. This problem can be viewed in its two aspects:- *(i)* the quantitative and *(ii)* qualitative. As regards the quantitative aspect is concerned, more secondary teachers and primary teachers per year would be required to meet the additional increase in primary and secondary schools. This would obviously mean huge expansion of training facilities and hence more of institutions.

This expansion if not wisely conducted is bound to lead to further deterioration in training. It is true that our education has remained unchanged even after independence. There is therefore, a great and urgent need not only to offset this deterioration that has taken place but also to strengthen our teacher education programme. Thus the following points need to be improved :

(1) Selection. There cannot be two opinions on the selection of teachers for training. For an important profession such as teaching, proper recruitment would be useful. Selection is a relative term. If the number of applicants is larger, some selection methods would be evolved and if the number of candidates is less, they have all to be admitted. The actual position is that some of the Government Training Colleges and a few good private institutions have selection methods while others have to find out trainees for their institutions.

Right type of students do not come forward for this profession. The intelligent and the superior candidates do not find the profession attractive. The third class students (barring a few exceptions) generally decide to become teachers because there are no other avenues for them.

Suggestions

(a) The minimum qualification for admission to B.Ed. should be second division in B.A., or B.Sc. degree. This may be relaxed in the case of M.A. and M.Scs.

(b) Marks in the subject of education could be a good indication of interest and success in the profession.

(c) Preference should be given to those who had taken up education as one of their subjects in their degree classes.

(d) Education should be introduced as an elective subject at the degree stage where there is no such arrangement.

(e) Interest, intelligence and aptitude tests should be given to the candidates.

(*f*) Proper interview can also reveal the right type of candidates for the profession.

(2) Integrated Teacher Training. There is a great need for an integrated programme of teacher education. At present there are a great variety of teacher training institutions in our country preparing teachers for different stages of education. It seems to be a wrong policy to compartmentalise teacher education programmes at different levels. Teacher education ought to be viewed as an integrated whole.

Suggestions

(*a*) Training of all types of teachers—elementary, secondary, science, craft, domestic science etc. should be under one roof to enhance the academic atmosphere of training of teachers.

(*b*) If for administrative reasons all the training classes cannot be conducted in one institution, these institutions with separate heads can be placed in one big campus, where they can easily coordinate their efforts.

(3) Teacher Training Programme. Our teaching methods have out-grown and hence training programmes are lifeless. The syllabi and the courses of instruction are completely out-of-date. They have failed to keep pace with modern ideas in education. Thare is no co-ordination between theory and practice. There is a greater emphasis on theory and less on practice teaching.

Suggestions

(*a*) Greater stress should be laid on the practical aspect of the training programme.

(*b*) New and practical methods of teaching should be evolved to suit Indian conditions.

(*c*) Love for the teaching profession should be cultivated among the teachers.

(*d*) The teaching practice should be on internship or apprenticeship basis for about three months during which the pupil teachers should be attached to a school as whole time teachers.

(*e*) Trainees should be encouraged to think critically on educational problems.

(4) Teacher Educators. Our training institutes are ill-staffed and understaffed. Owing to financial stringency they cannot maintain a proper and required student-teacher ratio. The staff members are over-loaded with work. Research work cannot be undertaken.

Suggestions

(*a*) There should be adequate staff because seminars, group discussions, paper reading and other jobs cannot be performed. Teaching without these would be useless.

(*b*) There should be at least one with Ph.D. qualification and others should be M.Ed.'s.

(5) Better in Service Facilities. It has been observed that newly trained teachers often forget what they have learnt in colleges of education as soon as they join schools. They follow the traditional method, may be for convenience sake or may be that old hands ridicule them. So in-service facilities should be provided to every trained teacher.

Suggestions

(*a*) To overcome the difficulty every teacher should be required to attend refresher short term courses at least once a year. This will brush up his knowledge.

A regular programme of in-service education of trained teachers in the field is necessary.

(*b*) Summer institutes during holidays should be organised.

(*c*) The present in-service facilities being inadequate need to be expanded by establishing an Extension Unit in every secondary training college.

(6) Need for Better Administration. Teacher education till now had been a neglected subject. At present it has been given some importance and hence accepted as Professional Education. But it is a pity that there is defect in administration and teacher education and it has not received that recognition which it deserves. The administration needs to be activised.

Suggestions

1. The Central Government should assume statutory responsibility for teacher education and establish a National Council for Teacher Education. It should be charged with the Planning work, Co-ordination and Maintenance of Teacher Education standards.

2. Similarly State Councils should be established for each state to pursue the work of Central National Council.

(7) Finance Requirement. The development of teacher education has suffered for paucity of funds. Most of training institutes are staggering and practically struggling for existence. Some of these do not justify their existence, being without adequate teaching staff, libraries hostel facilities etc.

Suggestions

1. Institutions without excellent arrangements should be better closed down than allowed to function in a poor way.

2. Better grant-in-aid should be given to these institutions enabling them to maintain the respectable desired standards.

(8) Need for Increasing Research and Publications. Training institutions should not be merely teaching shops. These are generally knowledge imparting centres. In the absence of good books, and professional literature for teachers and teacher educators, the standards of teaching have fallen. Books and journals which deal with the problems of education from Indian point of view are few.

Suggestions

1. Selected (efficient) training institutions should be asked to assume the literature production responsibility suited to Indian needs.

2. Research departments be added to really good institutions for research work. Arrangements should be made to publish the research investigations so that teachers may benefit.

(9) Need for Better Economic and Social Status. It is needless to say that the salary scales of our teachers have become a national scandal. A primary teacher in most of the states draws less than a peon of the central government and the pity is that he is called the nation builder. When teachers are so poorly paid, it is not possible to attract the right type of people to the profession.

Suggestions

1. Salary scales should be so revised as to ensured an honourable living.

2. Security of service should be guaranteed to them.

3. The economic status of teachers should be at least equal to that of equally qualified persons in other comparable professions.

(10) Training Wastage. Considerable amount of wastage is taking place in teacher training programmes. Quite a large number of students fail because of poor instruction. Some of the trained teachers finding their jobs less remunerative, give up the profession altogether. In the case of women teachers, there is still a greater wastage. They give up the profession after marriages or for other reasons like not getting a post at a secure place etc.

Suggestions

1. Evaluation techniques should be devised in such a way that minor wastage takes place.
2. Teachers' economic and social status should be raised.

(11) Status of Training Colleges. The status accorded to the training colleges is inferior. They are not considered on par with the post graduate institutions. This is obvious that the government have not realised the importance of teacher training centres. This leads to a doubtful status of the lecturers working in them.

Suggestions

Teachers deserve the status of post-graduate teachers because they teach the graduates and prepare them for a degree in education. They should be given all those facilities which teachers in post-graduate institutions enjoy.

Indian Education Commission 1882

The Indian Education Commission gave the following suggestions with regard to teacher education :

1. It urged the establishment of a number of training schools throughout the country.
2. Separate training arrangements for graduate and undergraduate teachers with separate courses of

training and syllabus. Towards the close of the 19th century, there were six training colleges and fifty six training schools for secondary teachers.

3. An examination in the theory and practice of teaching was recommended for secondary school teachers.

Government Resolution of 1914

1. Suggested highly qualified and trained teachers on the staff of training colleges.

2. There should be one year's training course for graduates and post-graduates leading to a degree and two years for under-graduates and others leading to teacher's certificate.

3. Training colleges should be suitably equipped.

4. A practising school should be attached to a training college.

On account of these recommendations, there was a great increase in the number of training institutions and better facilities for the trainees began to be offered.

Calcutta University Commission 1917

It laid stress on :

1. Increase in the output of trained teachers.

2. Creation of a department of education in the universities.

3. Systematising research work on training in the universities.

Hartog Committee Report 1929

It recommended that :

1. The standard of general education of Primary school teachers be raised.

2. Course of training be sufficiently long.
3. Arrangements for refresher courses and in service training be made for the trained teachers.

As a result of above recommendations, teacher training went on benefitting. The standard of training and consequently teaching improved considerably.

Recommendations of the Education Commission on Teacher Education

The Education Commission's recommendations on teacher education are of significant importance. It felt that in order to make the professional preparation of teachers effective, teacher education must be brought into the main stream of the academic life of the universities, on the one hand and school life and educational development on the other.

The following suggestions have been given by it :

1. *(a)* Schools of education should be established in selected universities to develop programmes in teacher education, studies and research in education.

(b) Extension work should be reorganised as an essential function of a teacher education institution and Extension Service Department be added to each institution.

(c) Organisation of student practice teaching in active collaboration with selected schools and these schools should receive substantial grants for equipment.

(d) Establishment of effective alumni associations to bring old students and faculty together to discuss and plan programmes and curricula.

(e) Recognition of education as an independent academic discipline and its introduction as an elective subject in the B.A., B.Sc., M.A. and M.Sc., degree courses.

(f) Establishing comprehensive colleges of education in each state on a planned basis.

(g) Arranging periodic exchange of the staff of the co-operating schools and of the teacher education institutions for the advantage of each category of staff.

2. *(a)* **Duration of the Course.** The duration of the professional courses should be two years for primary teachers who have completed the secondary school course and one year for the graduate students. The number of working days in a year should be increased to 230.

(b) **Flexible Post-Graduate Course in Education.** The post-graduate courses in education should be flexible and be planned to promote an academic and scientific study of education requiring special knowledge and initiative.

(c) **New Professional Courses.** New professional courses should be developed to orientate headmasters, teacher educators, educational administrators, to their special field of work.

3. **Improving Teacher Education Institutions.** *(a)* The staff of secondary training colleges should have a double Master's degree in academic subject and education, a fair proportion should hold doctorate degrees.

(b) Qualified specialists in psychology, sociology, science or mathematics may be appointed even if they have no professional training.

(c) Attempt should be made to recruit first and good second class students in teacher training institutions and adequate scholarships should be given to them.

(d) Summer Institutes should be organised for the in-service training of staff.

(d) All tuition fees in secondary teacher training institutions should be abolished and liberal provision made for stipends and loans.

4. Improving Professional Training. *(a)* Introducing integrated courses of general and professional education in universities.

(b) Using methods of study which leave greater scope for self study and discussion and methods of evaluation which include continuous internal assessment of practical and sessional work besides practice-teaching.

(c) Improvement of training institutions.

(d) Improving practice-teaching and making it a comprehensive programme of internship.

5. Expansion of Training Facilities. *(a)* Each State should prepare a plan for the expansion of teacher training facilities in its area to that the output of trained teachers meets the demand for teachers.

(b) Supplementary part time facilities should be provided on a large scale.

(c) The backlog of untrained teachers should be cleared during of the 4th Plan Period through suitable measures.

6. Professional Preparation of Teachers in Higher Education. *(a)* Some orientation is necessary for teachers in higher education and suitable arrangements should be made.

(b) Newly appointed lecturers should be given some time to adjust themselves to the institutions and should be encouraged to attend lectures of good teachers.

(c) Orientation courses for new staff should be organised in every university and where possible, in college.

7. Standards of Teacher Education. *(a)* The U.G.C. should take the responsibility at the national level for the maintenance of standards in teacher education.

(b) The U.G.C. should be given substantial funds in the 4th Plan for improvement in the teacher education.

(c) The U.G.C. should set up a standing committee for teacher education.

8. In-service Education. *(a)* Systematic and co-ordinated programmes of in-service education, in content and method, should be organised by universities.

(b) The programme of summer institutes for the in-service training of secondary school teachers should be extended with systematic follow-up.

❐

13

Adult Education

The movement of Adult Education in India is not very long past. The first impetus for the movement was given by the struggle for freedom that vigorously started in the beginning of the present century. Campaigns were organised to liquidate illiteracy among the masses. With the setting up of Congress Ministries in many states the movement gained a further momentum. In 1939 a Committee on Adult Education was appointed by the Central Advisory Board of Education (CABE) to survey the condition of illiteracy among the people. The Committee defined the objectives of Adult education as follows:

(a) teaching or 3 R's to the illiterates.

(b) imparting knowledge pertaining to the adult's working life.

Later, in 1944, C.A.B.E. laid emphasis on the first objective noted above and wanted that the function of Social Education may be placed in the background for some time to come. It said, "The main emphasis for some time to come should be on literacy although some provision should be made for adult education proper. Instruction must be intelligible to the non-literates and closely related to their occupations, personal interest and social and economic conditions. Adequate libraries should be provided".

After achieving Independence in 1947, greater stress began to be laid on social education, the objectives of which were improving, the standards of life and culture of the adult so that he might become a better citizen. The movement for liquidating illiteracy got a set-back as the result of this change in policy.

In 1949 the scheme of social education was taken up in hand on a large scale. The scattered attempts that had been made prior to this date had been quite successful. For example, Madras had organised libraries; West Bengal and Bihar had made arrangements for recreational and cultural activities; Bombay had experimented, successfully on Gram Shiksha Mohim. All these programmes had made an attempt to make the life of the adult healthier and happier. The Central government there designed to launch the movement of Social Education on a country-wide scale.

On the recommendation of the Education Commission (1964-66) a National Board of Adult Education was set up in 1970. The sorry state of affairs was disclosed in the first meeting of the Board by Professor V. K. R. V. Rao in the following words:

> "The percentage of literacy in India has increased from 6.2 to 33 during the period 1901 to 1969. But the number of illiterates has increased from 298 million in 1951 to 349 million in 1962. The illiteracy in the age group 15-44 is likely to be of a very great magnitude still".

The number of illiterates is swelling, though the percentage of literacy is going up every year. A programme of free and compulsory education has been stressed upon. It is considered to be the only strategy to make the masses literate. But the irony of fate is that the scheme of free and compulsory education has not been implemented successfully.

We have not yet been able to provide 5 years' schooling to every child. The system of primary education is still ineffective and wasteful. It is wasteful in the sense that "The child, who completes 5 years' schooling, either does not attain functional literacy or lapses into illiteracy soon after-wards". The implications are clear we cannot achieve universal literacy through this strategy alone even by 2000 A.D.

Such a drive is suggested because the campaigns launched so far to liquidate illiteracy on state basis have failed. The reasons why they could not achieve a desired success are:

(a) The campaigns were so limited in scale that it was difficult to achieve a significant advance.

(b) There are neither coordination nor collaboration among the agencies that attempted to liquidate illiteracy. Government departments, voluntary agencies, educational institutions, and individuals worked in isolation with one another.

(c) There was no planning. Neither were the needs and interests of the adults ascertained, nor was a public opinion aroused in its favour.

(d) There was no follow-up.

The national leadership has also been responsible for the slow progress in the field of adult education. The goal of universal literacy has been relinquished as unattainable. In its place, universal primary education has been emphasised. No national leader has ever considered the problem of education of illiteracy as an important one. Never in the history has priority been given to the cause of adult literacy. No political commitment has ever been made. The nation does not seem to realise the importance of adulated racy in matters of economic, growth and development of the country. Till the 150 million people in the age group 15-44 remain functionally illiterate, no one can think of achieving desired economic and social progress of the country.

Conceptual Framework of Adult Education

Adult Education is a broad concept involving literacy and social education. It is the responsibility of the state to increase the educational level of every citizen. It is in the interest of the society itself that proper education be provided not only to the children of a particular age group (say 11-14, 14-17) so that they become functionally literate and stop all further additions to the ranks of adult non-literates, but it is the moral obligation of the state to provide education to every adult, because education never ends with schooling.

Education is a life-long process and the education of the child and adolescent is but one course of action intended for a very small section of the society. The larger section consist of the adult members. And the adult of today more than before needs having a closer insight into the affairs of the rapidly changing world. A traditional society may be content with adults as they are. But a changing society and especially the one which has decided to bring about a revolution—social, cultural and intellectual—cannot remain satisfied with adults who lack the understanding of the present complexities of life. A nation which wants economic growth and development at a faster rate has to educate its adults in such a way that they participate in the developmental programmes intelligently willingly and effectively.

The importance of adult education to a developing country like India is much greater that to a developed country like England. Before 1947 though England had schemes of educating her adults, the British Government did not pay any attention to adult education in Indian. The significance of adult education (or further education) was realised when the country became free and launched programmes of planned economic development. It was now realised that the adult who tills the soil should know the nature of the soil and the worker who turns the lather should know the scientific process involved. The grown-up man or woman should know the implications of birth control and its importance in economy development. Each citizen has to save and preserve the security of the newly born nation.

The scope of adult education before 1947 was limited to universal adult literacy. The then national leadership wanted that all illiterate adults should be able to read and write so that they might understand what was happening in the country.

The aims of adult education have to be defined in reference to the political set-up of the country. "The chief function of adult education in a democracy", says the Education Commission (1964-66) "is to provide every adult citizen with an opportunity for education of the type which he wishes and which he should have for his personal enrichment professional advancement and effective participation in social and political life." Therefore with a change in the political set-up the aims of adults education changed. Before 1947 adult education remained confined to the liquidation of adult illiteracy. But after that date it was increasingly felt that the immediate objective of adult education should be the improvement in the standard of life and culture of the adult. So the concept of adult education underwent a change. The Central Advisory Board in its fifteenth meeting held in 1949 said, "In a democracy the provision of social education is all the more necessary, as without an educated electorate democracy cannot perform the functions expected of it. For this we want not mere literacy or mental development of the adults so that they can take an intelligent interest in the affairs of their country and the world."

Objectives of Social Education. A Committee was accordingly set up to define the objectives of social education under the chairmanship of Shri Mohan Lal Saxena. The

Committee gave a new orientation to the schemes of adult education. It said, "In view of far reaching implications of the scheme, it should be called a scheme for social education instead of a scheme for adult education. A new orientation must be given to schemes for the education of the adult. The immediate task is to improve the standards of life so that the adults may become a healthier, happier and better citizens. The work of literacy may go on, but even greater emphasis must be laid on the social aspect of education."

The sub-committee defined the objectives of social education as follows:

1. To give a reasonable mastery over the tools of learning, reading, writing, simple arithmetic and to create an interest in acquiring knowledge.

2. To develop a love for democracy and impart an understanding of the way in which democracy functions.

3. To infuse into the mind of the adult the sense of responsibility to the nation and to cherish a spirit of service to the community.

4. To provide facilities for continuation of education through libraries, discussion groups, clubs and institutions.

5. To produce fondness for cultural, heritage parting knowledge of historical facts and conditions.

6. To instruct adults in simple laws and principles of personal health and hygiene.

7. To give an insight into the problems faced by the country and the world at large.

8. To train them in some craft so that they may better the economic condition.

9. To provide cultural and recreational facilities by way of music, drama, poetry recitation, folk songs, folk dances and other ways of self-expression.

The above list of objectives is however not exhaustive. In any scheme of social education all those activities will find place which lead to the economic, cultural and social growth of the adult. The schemes of social education, therefore, do not place so much emphasis on producing the ability for reading and writing in the non-literate adult. Literacy is only one aspect of social education. Social education, in wider sense, implies "a comprehensive approach to the solution of the problems of the community, primarily through community action." In this sense a programme of social education is a correlate of community development programmes.

The social education programmes include the entire national extension and community development programmes, social welfare extension projects, rural uplift work undertaken by government agencies in cooperation with the people. Activities of voluntary organisations like Bharat Sewak Samaj, Sarva Sewa Sangh and others, the cooperative movement and the village panchayats are also included in the schemes of social education.

Concept of Functional Literacy

Literacy means ability to read and write. Literacy as such, is one of the basic elements of education. Literacy to be worthwhile should be not formal but functional. A functionally literate person is one who has mastery over the reading and writing skills and at the same time has knowledge enough to pursue his own, interests and purposes. A functionally literate person is able to assume social, civic and economic roles in life that make him a happier, healthier and abler citizen. The rudimentary literacy training consists of teaching of reading and writing only, whereas the functional literacy training is comprised in imparting knowledge pertinent to the pursuit of one's interests and ends. The rudimentary literary training is simply a means to functional literacy.

The concept of functional literacy has to be distinguished from the concept of adult literacy. Adult literacy simply means teaching the non-literate adult the skills of reading and writing so that he may be able to acquire knowledge and information immediately needed in the improvement of the standard of life.

The concept of functional literacy is very well explained in the report of the World Conference of Education Ministers on the Eradication of Illiteracy be U.N.E.S.C.O. (1959) which says: "The process of learning to read and write should be made an opportunity for acquiring information that can immediately be used to improving living standards. Reading and writing should not only lead to elementary general knowledge but to training for work, increased productivity, a greater participation in civic life, a better under-standing of the surrounding world and should open the way to basic human culture."

The programmes of functional literacy are conducted at three stages. In the first stage, the non-literates are taught the 3 R's and they are introduced to civic and national problems and to the profession they are engaged in. In the second stage, the skills of reading and writing are strengthened. The stress is laid on the depth of knowledge gained in the first stage. In the last stage, they are directed to programmes of continuing or further education.

The aims and objectives of these programmes are:

1. enabling the non-literate adult to read and write.
2. creating favourable attitudes for and interest in one's own occupation.
3. empowering him to play an effective role in the social and political life of the country.

4. inspiring him to use the knowledge of 3 R's for further education.
5. imparting skills and information to perform his work efficiently.

The functional literacy programmes impart not only literacy and numeracy to the non-literates, but they enable them to continue their education either through available agencies of informal education or through their own private efforts. They are generally work-based so that the trainee becomes efficient in the work he is engaged in. In the social education programmes more emphasis is laid on inculcating social and civic values in the adult. The primary objective of social education programmes is creation of effective citizens for a democracy.

Adult Literacy and National Development

Illiteracy is a curse to the individual and to the society. The illiterate or the non-literate lives a life of oblivion. In so many ways his existence is inferior to that of the literate or the educated one. There is little prospect of a reasonable income. Sophisticated social graces are denied to him. He cannot take any part in a democratic government. Illiteracy as a mass phenomenon is a bane to the society. It puts obstacles in the way of social and economic progress. Economic productivity is materially affected. Schemes of population control are set at naught.

Illiteracy resists social change. The non-literates tend to cling to traditional ways of life. New ideas and new practices cannot be effectively communicated to minds which are untrained to receive them. Whether it is family planning or improvements of sanitary standards or any other programme of social security it will not make any sense to the illiterate people.

The illiterate man does not make a democracy. He does not understand the duties and responsibilities of citizenship in a democracy. He is liable to be misled by evil propaganda. Democracies do not flourish on uneducated electrorates.

In a country, which has adopted a socialistic democratic pattern of life and has determined to achieve economic development in the shortest time possible, it is very necessary that the entire population should become functionally literate. "Without adult education and adult literacy," says Professor V.K.R.V. Rao, "it is not possible to have that range and spread of economic and social development which we require nor is it possible to have that content or quality or tone to our economic and social development that makes it worth-while in terms of values and welfare. A programme of adult education and adult literacy should therefore take a front place in any programme of social and economic development."

Under the stress of circumstances a massive unorthodox national movement has to be started to liquidate illiteracy in the age group of 14-44 and provide adult education to all. 'The nation-wide sustained programme has to be organised and supported vigorously by social and political leadership, by state and central governments, by educational institutions of all types and grades. All the employees working in large firms, commercial, industrial, contractors are not functionally literate. If they are given proper training in the 3 R's. if they are introduced to skills and information needed for the job in hand, they will be able to produce more. All adults whether they are working in a firm or a farm should be made to participate in the developmental programmes willingly, intelligently and efficiently. The farmer who tills the soil and handles the plough must know the nature of the soil and the efficiency of tools. The worker who is turning a lather must know how to adjust the machine. Both of them must understand the scientifiic processes involved in production-agricultural or industrial.

The country needs modernisation of agriculture. It needs a faster industrial, development. But how can it be possible to accelerate the pace of economic development with two-thirds or even more of its workforce as illiterate or functionally non-literate?

Organising and Administering Adult Education. No system can work to fruition unless it is properly organised and administered. We must first establish suitable bodies at all levels—the school, the block the district, the state and the centre to look after the work of adult education and adult literacy. A National Board of Adult Education can be set up at the Centre to advise the Centre and the states in matters concerning adult education. The functions of the Board would be coordinating the efforts of different ministries, and of official and non-official agencies, reviewing the progress achieved, formulating policies and promoting research in the filed.

Libraries will have to be strengthened at all levels and amply stocked with reading materials beneficial to new-literates, good and useful enough to attract aduts. Universities may also help a great deal in furthering the cause of adult education.

Programmes of Adult Education

The Education Commission has suggested to develop the following programmes of adult education on a priority basis:

Liquidating Illiteracy. It has been analysed in a previous section why there has been a slow progress in the field of adult education. The growth of population at an unprecedented fast rate has brought down the pace of progress in adult literacy during the last two decades. There were more non-literates in 1961 than in 1951 : there were more literates in 1971 than in 1961. The number of non-literates, in spite of vigorous attempts to fulfill the Constitutional Directive as early as possible, is on the increase. A massive all-round national effort is needed to achieve universal literacy.

A planned programme for liquidating illiteracy involves following steps:

1. expanding universal free primary education for age group 6-11.
2. providing part-time education to children in age group 11-14 who either drop out prematurely or miss schooling.
3. providing part-time general and vocational education to adults of age group 15-30.
4. liquidating illiteracy among older adults 30-44, through a selective or mass approach.

1. Expanding free compulsory primary education for the age group 6-11 has been the sole strategy during the first three five year plans and much has been achieved through them. The boys and girls who drop from schools after receiving their primary education either lapse into illiteracy or become functionally non-literate.

2. For young adults, who have passed the high school examination but cannot continue education further, part-time courses may be offered to pass the higher secondary examination and part-time professional courses may be organised for those who have joined agriculture or industry or some trade or who want to be self-employed.

3. Some boys and girls, who have completed their primary schooling and passed the middle school stage, are not able to continue their education on a full-time basis but want to prepare for the high school examination at the end of class X; opportunities should be provided to them in the same school, under the same teachers with the same equipment.

There may be others in this group who have actually adopted some career and desire to improve their professional efficiency.

4. For adults above 30 years of age who are non-litarates two types of programmes have been suggested selective and mass approach programmes. Under selective approach, for groups of employees working in large firms, commercial, industrial or otherwise functional literacy may be regarded as the responsibility of the employers. The Education Commission recommended that the work of liquidating illiteracy in the public sector industrial plants may be forthwith taken up by the Government agencies.

Under the mass approach of liquidating illiteracy every educated man and woman should be required to teach at least one man or woman. 'Teach one each one' programme may be mobilized again. Teachers, students and all educational institutions should participate under obligation in a well-planned literary campaign. Every educated person should think it to be his duty to the nation to combat illiteracy.

The Central Social Welfare Board has done commendable work for liquidating illiteracy among woman folk. Condensed courses have been started for training village sisters who are teaching village woman reading and writing. Such courses may be started and woman village teachers may be trained on a large scale.

Present State of Adult Education. Adult Education no longer means liquidation of illiteracy. The idea of traditional litetracy in the 3 R's has been left aside and the country has launched a comprehensive programme of an all round development of the adult. The changing social economic scene demands such an over-all development of human resources. Elementary education is being universalised and at the same time the adult population is given all sort of educational facilities so that their educational depreciation may be remedied and their potentiality may be developed.

On the one hand the governments, the state and central both have waged a clearly conceived, well planned and relentless struggle against illiteracy so that the masses may be able to play an active role in social and cultural change. Literacy is now regarded as the vital part of an individuals pleasingly. And the development of the personality of the adult means his ability to read and write well.

On October 2, 1978 a National Adult Education Programme has been launched and by 1983-84 it aims at providing facilities to 10 crores of illiterate persons in the age group 15-35. The main objectives of the Programme are:

(a) Development of the country's human resources in the vital age group 15-35.

(b) Creating social awareness among the illetrate masses.

(c) Provision of basic literacy skills.

(d) Upgrading of functional skills.

The following bodies have been set up to implement the policies effectively.

(a) A National Board of Adult Education to advise the Central Government in the formulation of policies.

(b) District Level Committees to ensure proper coordination and examing the implementation of the programme at the local level.

(c) Voluntary organisations.

(d) State Boards of Adult Education to advise the state governments.

Continuing Education. It has been stated earlier in this section that those who are desirous of continuing education for the stage they have not been able to receive education in the school, part-time teaching may be provided in the same school by the same teaches (with due allowance for extra work done). Here we want to stress that besides such opportunities for part-time education, parallel part-time system of education may be started in schools, factories and farms. Doors of educational institutions of all types and grades should be kept open to those who are desirous of getting education in them. Opportunities should be created for desirous adults to earn the same certificates, degrees and diplomas as are received by regular students. For example the Directorate of Delhi has started Adult Education Centres in some of the same buildings in which Higher Secondary Schools run. But the classes are taken in the evening and provisions for teaching those boys and girls are made who being employed somehow cannot attend day schools.

Factories may start education centres in their own premises for teaching their own workers. In this way they may increase the knowledge, improve skills, widen horizons in life and improve the careers of their employees.

Similar opportunities may be provided by larger firms to their employees to get further education in the work they are doing.

❐

14

Promotion of Education

According to the Kothari Commission, in India the problem of educational planning means simply that we need to evolve a national policy in the educational sphere while, according to our Constitution, education is a state subject, and consequently, educational officials at various levels take decisions on all of its varied aspects. The task before us is not simple, and we also do not have much experience to guide us. Hence, we will have to evolve our own techniques, and change, modify and improve them as we go along.

The following are the elements of a comprehensive educational plan which have to be improved in order to overcome the problems that arise in the educational sphere:

1. Creation of literature in the modern Indian languages, which is necessary for making these languages the medium of instruction at the university level.
2. Educational Research.
3. Improvements in the system of examination.
4. Preparation of text-books for schools and help-materials for teaching and study.
5. Arrangements for the in-service training of teachers and officials of the education department.

6. Improvements in the methods of supervision.
7. Provision of progressive schemes for brilliant students and programmes of special assistance to backward students.
8. Increase in the contact with guardians and the local community.

Obstactes in the way

The results of education can be good only if educational planning is successful. In our country, educational planning faces the following obstacles :

1. Excessive emphasis upon enrolment and expenditure.
2. Decentralisation of efforts.
3. Indifference towards accepting clearly defined paths of action.
4. Weakness of the educational planning mechanism.
5. Failure to initiate programmes of superior quality.
6. Absence of adequate evaluation and research.

The Planning Commission's Working Group on education has identified the following causes of the failure of planning:

1. Administration of the police kind, obsolete methods, inadequate resources, increased responsibilities of development, and untrained, incapable and inadequate staff.
2. Proper utilisation of resources is hindered because of lack of resources, lack of extension schemes, delays in obtaining financial clearance, changes in the proposed amounts or corrupt activities.

3. Lack of attraction for trained individuals; tradition of making appointments from above; absence of any system of in-service training; excessive emphasis upon individual and financial administration. There is need for a revolutionary change in the nature and structure of the states department of education. Instead of functioning as groups of individuals concerned with grants, statistics, financial permission, transfers, appointments, study of complaints, etc., these groups have to become organisations of educationists which possess the imagination to visualise the objectives of educational reconstruction, which are sensitive enough to recognise quickly the needs and demands of people immediately, which can prepare satisfactory plans for reconstruction and implement them successfully, which can fulfil the roles of friends, philosophers and guides for the teachers as well as students and their guardians.

4. Wherever suitable leadership has been found lacking, democratic decentralisation has led either to the obstruction of educational schemes or a complete and destructive change in their very nature. Local influences and force often create problems for the teachers.

5. The entire society is responsible for making the educational plan successful. Till the present, there is no effective system for establishing contact between teachers, students, guardians educational administrators and the rest of society, though the existence of such a system is a prime necessity.

6. Co-operation and harmony with other governmental departments and non-governmental agencies is weak and ineffective.

7. The thought that goes into making a budget or preparing in a plan is the equivalent of a kind of evaluation. Evaluation is made from time to time. The discussion in the organisations of teachers, the press and the legislative assemblies are also forms of evaluation. But, hardly any efforts have been made so far towards introducing a systematic and formal mode of evaluation by individuals directly involved in education.

8. Political pressures are often seen working powerfully in the appointment and transfer of teachers, setting up of new institutions and location of schools. The same pressures also influence and modify approved schemes.

In view of these factors, the Working Group felt constrained to say that comprehensive educational plans, keeping in view every aspect of education, should be prepared. The existing situation is that the states' departments of education thrust the responsibility for planning on certain officials, who then prepare plans and programmes without getting into touch with anyone. Specialists, teachers, organisations of teachers, or educational officials of the district level make no contribution to such plans. Besides, these plans are full of statistics about goals of appointments and expenses, while other much more important aspects of education are completely neglected.

Detailed schemes and blue-prints are also required for the successful implementation of a plan. No attention is paid to this fact. The Working Group's view is that educational programmes should be treated in the same way in which projects concerning irrigation, industry or power are treated. We should see not merely the clarity of objectives; we must also seek to ensure the achievement of these objectives by considering the time division, need for preparatory work, materials expenditure needed for creating the necessary skills and motivation and administrative requirements, and then try to harmonise them with the time available and conditions existing. At present, there is a complete absence of such projects. It seems that detailed thinking does not go into the preparing of plans by the education ministry and the Planning Commission, and after plans are once prepared, re-thinking occurs only after a year has passed. Assessments are hardly ever made. Besides, the various agencies looking after education also lack coordination among themselves. At the National level, various ministries, such as food, agriculture, labour, social welfare, home, etc, are also involved in educational planning. Similar agencies exist in the states also, but the co-ordination among them is quite weak.

It is true that education is the state's responsibility, but it cannot be denied that the nation has an equal responsibility as well as stake in the success of education. Hence, the states and the centre should be regarded as equal partners in education. There are three main agencies of education—*(i)* the central government, *(ii)* the state governments, and *(iii)* local bodies and voluntary organisations. Besides, it is evident that *(a)* school education involves the partnership of the local government and the state government, and *(b)* higher education is conducted through the partnership of the state and central governments. A balance can be struck between complete centralisation or decentralisation after these truths are recognised and accepted.

The Working Group has offered the following suggestions for making educational planning successful:

1. Preparation of Comprehensive Educational Plans. Allocation of resources is all that is actually being done in the name of formulating plans. A comprehensive educational plan is inclusive of the existing situation in education, the objectives, of education, the steps to be taken for achieving these objects, all programmes, those which involve no expenditure or those for which expenditure has to be reduced, etc.

2. Introduction of Institutional Plans. The basic principle of this new technique will be institutional plans, *i.e.*, plans prepared by the schools themselves. At the school level, plans have to be formulated by considering what can be done within the available resources or by adding a little to them. Good schools in particular should work in this direction.

Basis of the Process of Planning

The second necessary reform relates to giving the planning process a wider basis and decentralising it, as well as bringing about co-ordination between the institution, district, state and centre. This will produce a wide range of advantages.

Work can be started in the states on the basis of the following suggestions :

1. An essential condition for granting recognition and aid should be that each school should prepare a five-year plan, as well as annual plans, for its own development.
2. These plans should also become the basis of inspection.
3. The department of educational should provide some guidelines in the preparation of the school's plan which should be clearly in consonance with the state's policy on education.
4. The state educational institution should train principals as well as inspectors.
5. Long-term plans will run concurrently with the state's five-year plans. Schools will re-open at the fixed

time, though students will attend school a week latter. During this period, the teachers will consider every aspect of teaching and prepare plans for the forthcoming session.

6. All the related agencies—teachers, students, society, guardians, principal, the management committee, etc., should participate in the preparation of the plan.
7. Inspectors should receive detailed information about plans and evaluation well in advance.
8. Inspectors often compel schools to adopt many schemes simultaneously. For this, it is essential that the schemes should be limited in range, and they should be completed before others are taken up.

We should remember that education is a never-ending or inexhaustible source of personal satisfaction. It is related directly to the nation's social and economic development. If education is systematically initiated at every level, and if it is intimately related to national programme, the pace of social and economic development increases.

Governmental Planning

While reflecting upon institutional planning, we are faced with the following questions—*(i)* What are your objectives? *(ii)* Is it our purpose to work for the achievement of new objectives? *(iii)* Do we want to bring about a change in individuals? *(iv)* Is it our purpose to replace the old patterns with fresh ones? These questions imply that our thinking on the issue should be clear. The function of institutional planning is to keep an institution occupied in the search for the best possible results in the existing social environment.

In the context of formulating a plan with clear objectives for any institution, it is necessary to reflect upon the existing circumstances. One cannot turn away from the realities of life and society. We must overlook the fact that our universities are tradition bound and that they have to work according to the directives of the department of education. It is the department which formulates the curriculum and also issues orders about its implementation. Thus, if we can still think of an imaginative plan for a particular institution, despite the existence of these circumstances, it must necessarily be appreciated.

In order to prepare an educational plan for a single institution, it is necessary to consider the following basis:

1. Making the best use of the talents of the students and teachers.
2. Achievement of the best possible results in the given social and physical environment.
3. Generating a suitable atmosphere for the development of creativity.
4. Reform and progress in technique, materials, resources, etc.
5. Recognition of innate powers, their use, encouragement of efforts and leadership.
6. Achieving the maximum utilisation of building, laboratories, libraries and other resources.
7. Encouraging mutual co-operation without injuring freedom of thought and action.

The Working Group of the Planning Commission has suggested the following means of bringing success to the plans of schools :

1. The states' departments of education will have to begin to think a new in order to recognise or identify good schools and grant them greater aid as well as

freedom, to guide the weaker schools towards improvement, and also to encourage competitiveness, creativity and experimentation amongst teachers and students.

2. Teachers have necessarily to shoulder the leadership in the formulation and implementation of institutional plans. Among primary schools, there exists the peculiar problem of single-teacher institutions. For such cases, all institutions within a radius of three to five miles will treat the higher secondary school as the centre, and function as a school complex, and their institutional plan will also be a collective one. From the viewpoint of organisation, each complex should be treated as a unit. At the secondary school level, the form of principals will work to achieve co-operation from the nearest college or university and to ensure mutual co-operation.

3. The schools themselves should try to secure the means needed for their development. The best steps in this direction would be *(i)* the co-operation of local officials, guardians and the local community, *(ii)* a change in the method of giving grants in order to encourage superiority, and *(iii)* establishment of experimental schools and autonomous colleges.

4. It is necessary to initiate co-operation and mutual dialogue between schools and colleges, instead of allowing them to throw allegations at each other. School complexes can be of tremendous advantage in this sphere.

5. Transfers of teachers in government schools should be reduced to a minimum. Organising committees or boards of governors should be created, and in these the teachers should have an important voice,

so that their commitment should be to the institution, and not merely to their cadre. Such a situation does not exist in private institutions, and hence they should make efforts to attract the best teachers towards themselves.

6. Colleges will, in general, not have much difficulty in preparing their own plans, but they can seek the guidance of the university. The universities, too, will frame their own plans. For this purpose, in keeping with the suggestions of the Education Commission, they will create their own 'academic planning boards.'

7. Transfers can help each other in the framing and implementation of plans even through the method of Panel Inspection. The panel can consist of some selected teachers and principals who can give the benefit of their experience and knowledge to other institutions, apart from their own, by giving a little extra time.

Different Levels

Institutional planning operates at three levels—*(1)* District, *(2)* State and *(3)* National.

1. District Level Plans. Accepting the district as the fundamental unit of planning, development and administration, work is to be initiated in some districts in the next year itself. It is to be introduced in every district by the end of the sixth five year plan. Today, the expenditure on education in a single district is more than the total expenditure in India in 1882. The educational plan of a district should comprehend all educational activity below the level of university education, pre-primary, primary; secondary and vocational. Towns with a population of a lakh or more can also have their separate plans, in which the municipal boards should also offer co-operation.

2. State Level Plans. Plans at the state level have to become the centre of gravity of the entire planning process, and for this purpose, it is essential that every state department of education must have a powerful and effective planning will. For the near future, the following programmes have been suggested for immediate implementation: *(i)* Evaluation of the development from independence till the present, *(ii)* formulation of a long term plan for fifteen or twenty years, publication of a white paper on the subject, and giving it a final shape in the light of the suggestions received, *(iii)* framing of an education Act.

3. National Plans. At the national level, the government of India has suggested the formulation of a national educational policy which should be reviewed every five years. National plans will be based on this national policy. Their main elements will be the following: *(i)* the synthesizing element of framing a national plan based on all state-plans, *(ii)* co-ordinated action on the national plan by the centre as well as the states, *(iii)* central programmes to be implemented either by constitutional directives or the assent of the states. It will be the Centre's responsibility to produce a plan which does away with regional differences, which is balanced, and which is suited for a long tenn period.

The Dual Process of Plan Formulation. Planning has to be done both from above and from below. It is necessary to have two time-tables in the planning process. For example, guidelines and hints about the temporary allocation of resources will flow from the central government to the state government, from the state government to the district level officials and institutions. In the reverse process, the institutions will prepare their own plans in the light of the information given. They will indicate the plans they can implement with the given resources, and what they may be able to do if more resources are made available, etc.

Contribution of Teachers. Teachers are expected to co-operate intimately and effectively in educational plans. Theoretically, this does not appear to be an unusual idea, but in effect, it has been implemented so far because of the following four factors : *(i)* The government has never shown any interest in this, and in fact the government has never understood either this problem or its importance. *(ii)* We have, as yet, never seen even a dream of any institutional organisation which makes it possible for teachers to participate in the formulation and implementation of educational plan. *(iii)* There are so many differences among the various categories of teachers that the whole profession has been weakened, and consequently the teacher's capacity to contribute to educational planning is almost destroyed. *(iv)* Teachers are also lacking in specialisation and leadership, besides which they have adopted an attitude of indifference towards the problems of education planning. These four difficulties have to be overcome in order to benefit education by raising the status of teachers, which can be done by giving them the leadership in educational planning and development.

For this, the following suggestions have been offered:

(i) School-planning should be introduced in every school.

(ii) At the district level, there should be an advisory board council of teachers on which every teacher's organisation of the district should have representation. It should be consulted in every matter pertaining to educational planning and development.

(iii) The Central ministry of education should establish a national committee of teachers on which every teacher organisation of the national level should be re-

presented. In planning and development matters, this committee should be consulted, as is to be done at the district and state levels.

(iv) The government should declare, without any reservations and conditions, that it wishes to hand over the leadership in matters of educational planning to the teachers, and, that the responsibility for helping in this work and collecting the necessary resources will fall upon the department of education. Such a declaration will influence the attitudes of departmental officials as well as teachers and lead to the creation of a suitable environment which is essential for the success of this entire programme.

(v) The teachers themselves should develop an interest in planning. It is unfortunate that teachers have neglected this important aspect of their vocation. Teachers organisations have shown no interest in the past three five year plans and three annual plans. They have not indulged in any profound criticism or analysis, though it is expected of them that they would not only subject the government's plans to criticism, but also offer a parallel plan of their own, so that the people may have an opportunity for a comparative study. It is obvious that teachers will have to give up this indifference, and the sooner it is done, the better.

(vi) Similar advisory boards should also be created at the, state level, and these should be called joint teachers' councils.

(vii) If teachers of all categories unite and form a single, organised community, their contribution to educational administration can become more effective. For this, the first thing necessary is a change of attitude. At present, the teaching profession is divided into a number of discrete units which, it appears, visit their own classrooms individually without ever entering into a working relationship. It is obvious that there is no place for such at alienated outworn attitude in the new India that we dream of, a country with a social system based on equality, freedom, justice and the dignity of the individual. The community of teachers is one, and all within it are fundamentally equal.

(vii) Efforts must be made to win the co-operation of the teachers in administrative activities relating to the school as well as other matters.

(ix) Teachers will also have to develop the necessary skills for planning; both individuals and in groups, through their organisations. Of course, it is true that this will happen only when the plan for decentralisation outlined earlier is implemented and teachers are asked to cooperate.

(x) In order to generate a commitment among the teachers for the institutions in which they teach, it is essential for them to have an effective voice in its administration. Suitable efforts for this will have to be made in private as well as governmental institutions.

Training

It is necessary to train all individuals concerned with the formulation and implementation of plans. Besides, some selected individuals must also be specially trained for formulating and implementing certain specialised projects. A detailed document should be prepared for each scheme, showing the objectives, period of work, finance, individuals involved, description of resources, arrangements for co-ordination, a detailed time division plan, made of evaluation, preparatory work, etc. This task is undoubtedly difficult, and the specialists available will also be few. Hence, the Asian Educational Planning and Administration Institution can be entrusted with providing help in this sphere.

Eradication of the Stress on Money

Every effort should be made to get rid of the stress on money in educational plans. If we imagine that surplus funds will help us to end every conceivable problem in education, the idea only indicates our naivette. After spending substantial amounts of money we have succeeded in expanding the general system of education and in creating new institutions, better scales of pay for teachers, more teaching, putting up more buildings, and expansion of resources. However, those improvements which were not related with finance have met with limited success only. We have almost completely failed in the growth of adult literacy or in preventing wastages and stagnation in primary education. The enrolment at the university and secondary level has not decreased. No noticeable progress in the schemes for qualitative improvement has been noted. For all these activities, what is needed is more and better human resources, not more money. In the sphere of human efforts, our work has been unsatisfactory. In a rich country, the emphasis upon money may not mean a serious loss, but in a poor country like ours, this lavishness is intolerable. We can achieve success in our objectives if we adopt the following major programmes along with our other schemes :

1. Intensive Use of Available Resources. Efforts should be made to derive the maximum profits from the existing investments, instead of seeking avenues for fresh investments.

2. Research on Inexpensive Techniques. Science should pay attention to this field.

3. Selective Technique. Instead of taking up numerous schemes simultaneously some selected schemes should be chosen on the basis of priorities.

4. Human Efforts. The vicious circle lack of education in a poor country itself becoming the cause of further poverty should be broken through enthusiastic and dedicated human effort.

5. Priorities. It is necessary to determine priorities at the national, state and local levels. Today, there is a tendency to think of everything in terms of the national level. Instead of this attitude, it would be better if, at the national level, priority is given only to some subjects of truly national importance. These can be treated as national schemes. In teaching, production of books and teaching of science can be treated as national schemes for the sixth plan. On these issues, the Centre should finalise decisions after consultation with the states.

On most of the remaining issues, the states themselves must take their own decisions, and in accordance with local needs determine the priorities. For instance, at the secondary level, the question of an educational fee can be taken up. There is no need to seek uniformity at the national level in such matters. In many other matters, such as facilities in schools and non-teacher costs, priorities will have to be fixed at the local level, in consonance with local needs and the clearly defined rights and authority of the school or local body, which should also have the necessary freedom to take decisions. There is no need to expect absolute uniformity in all districts: In some matters, freedom must be given even to the schools. Neither is there any need to accept complete uniformity and conformity in all schools of the same category. A system based on co-ordinated and rationally determined priorities separately determined, at the national, state and local levels will be far better than the prevailing system in which, so far, many decisions have been taken, even in matters of regional and national importance, without the least attention to local needs. Such a system has led to the complete obstruction of any tendency to take the initiative and bring improvements. What is needed is relatively better coordination and harmony between all the agencies, departments and ministries concerned with education, rather than any attempt to foist an unnecessary uniformity.

Reforms in Administration

For the proper implementation of educational programmes, it is necessary to bring about improvements in educational administration on the basis of well-defined priorities. At present, the education department focuses its attention only upon maintaining organisational administ-ration, with the result that the duty of developmental administration is not fulfilled at all. For this latter purpose, the departments of education should have full knowledge of educational programmes in all the states of our own country as well as. the programmes initiated in foreign countries. Besides they should give suitable importance to all such programmes in their own educational planning, keeping in view the needs, aspirations and ambitions of the people of their region. Such a developmental administration will possess the following characteristics:

1. The existing organisational administration soon becomes involved in its own web of ever-expanding rules and regulations, by laying excessive stress upon control. It is thus unable to spare a thought to progress or development. In contrast, developmental administration gives importance to the independence of teachers and institutions, expansion in extension services and guidance, experimentation, initiative and creativity, and encourages all of them.

2. Organisational administration is suitable for a static or slowly progressing society, because it always sticks to uniformity and insists on obedience to rules. On the other hand, developmental administration concerns itself with the development of the individual in a rapidly changing society, and for this purpose, it does not hesitate to modify its own policy, if this is necessitated by circumstances.

3. Developmental administration accords equal importance to the twin aspects of quantitative and qualitative improvement in education. It makes continuously modifiable and improved schemes for the future, evaluates the experiences of the past and present, and simultaneously provides the administrators with ever increasing opportunities for increasing their professional skills.

4. Developmental administration is completely democratic and decentralised. As is the case of organisational administration, it has no place for the centralisation of power or the creation of a bureaucratic approach. Every individual, at every level, has the right to make rules, to work accordingly and to evaluate his activities.

5. Another drawback of organisational administration is that it creates the two classes of teachers and administrators, with greater benefits invariably flowing to the latter. This discrimination invariably has an adverse impact both upon the teacher and the teaching process, as well as development of education. In contrast, developmental administration invariably aims at healthy relations between the two classes so that both of them are able to fulfil their respective duties without coming into conflict with each other.

Having been accustomed to organisational administration for almost centuries it now appears difficult to adopt developmental administration. Even today, our administration spends almost the whole of its time in the appointment of workers, their transfers, promotions and investigation into anonymous complaints and allegations. Whatever time does remain is spent in sorting out financial complications. The consequence of this is that the department soon loses all touch with society, and it turns into an isolated tower standing in a waste land. In order to introduce developmental administration, we will first have to overcome these drawbacks. The suggestions for the improvement of educational administration are based on our assumption that the central and state governments are faced with the major task of making the objectives of education determined by the governments themselves.

Part Time Education

The second very significant programme far important is the provision of in-service education for educational administrators. This is even more important in view of the fact that the condition of the states' departments of education is truly pitiable at present. For this, the following steps have been suggested :

1. Each administrator or inspector should be required, on being first appointed, to complete a course of training, whose period and subject should be in accord with the posts held by the individual.

2. Education of this kind should have two purposes—one, to acquaint the officials from time to time with the states' educational policies, and two; to get an opportunity to study improvements in education in India and abroad and to assess them in the light of the conditions in their own state. These officials should participate in conferences or seminars or

workshops for at least a week twice a year. Such conferences should be organised, at the district or regional level, by the district officials, for the non-gazetted staff, while for the gazetted staff, they should be organised by the director of education.

3. Officials of one state should be sent to other states for studying particular problem.

4. Each department should regularly publish a newspaper or letter of the highest quality in order to acquaint its officials with the latest government policies as well as the least thinking in the educational sphere by leading educationists.

5. Both at the national and state levels, there should be arrangements by which officials of other departments concerned with education and its problems can be kept in touch with latest ideas, and also be given training.

6. It is essential to have provisions for granting leave to those officials who wish to improve their knowledge or enter specialised studies at regular intervals. Six months leave can be granted after every six years for such purposes.

7. The ministry of education, the NCERT, and the Asian Educational Planning and Administration Institute should prepare programme for in-service training, since such a programme can bring to the participants the knowledge, experience and guidance of experts and scholars in ,this field. The states' departments of education should allow their officials to participate in such programmes freely.

The Kothari Education Commission had suggested the establishment of a National College for the training of educational administrators. This is a very valuable suggestion, and it should be accepted and implemented in, the present plan-period. Giving opportunities for improving professional qualifications is a good idea, but not all individuals are able to benefit from them. Hence, for encouragement, they should also be given incentives, such as promotions or increase in pay. In view of the existing circumstances, it is essential that, within the next one or two years, massive programmes for the reorientation of our educational administrators should be taken up. In all such programmes organised at the national, regional or local level, the states and the Centre should co-operate with each other.

Programme for Growth

The third programme for the improvement of educational administration concerns the proper organisation of developmental work regarding schools and workers. For the last twenty years, our attention has been focused upon the quantitative expansion of education, but the time is now ripe for concentrating upon its qualitative improvement. Many elements are important for this, for instance—the abilities of teachers, their devotion to duty, the commitment and motivation of students, an atmosphere conducive to truth and hard work, provision of facilities, a developed curriculum, dynamic methods of teaching and evaluation, research, good supervision and guidance work, and a favourable social climate. However, solving the problems of educational administration depends upon two factors—*(i)* school organisation, and *(ii)* supervision and guidance.

Before 1947, educational authorities were compelled to bear two burdens, those of administration as well as introduction of programmes of qualitative improvement. But after 1950, the work load of administrative activities upon these officers increased to such an extent that they had almost no time to spare for programme of qualitative improvement.

Even as early as 15 years ago, it was felt that there was need for establishing special agencies to carry out developmental programmes. It was with this in view that such institutions as the Central Text-book Research Bureau, the Central Educational and Vocational Guidance Bureau, the National Audio-visual Education Institution, the National Basic Education Institute, the National Institute of Primary Education, Directorate for Extension Programmes in Secondary Education, Central English and Hindi Institutes, etc., were established. In a similar fashion, in the states, too, state education institutes audio-visual education institutes, educational and, vocational guidance institutes, evaluation organisations, state science teaching institutes, and the English institute, etc., came to be established.

On the basis of past experience, the following suggestions can be offered for bringing about qualitative improvement :

1. So far, universities have remained completely cut off from schools. Now, they should offer their co-operation for the improvement of school education through research, improved curricula, search for new and better methods of teaching and evaluation, teacher training, preparation of superior text-books, etc.

2. In the organisation of the above institutions, those professionally skilled individuals should be appointed who can understand the problems of school education, seek solutions to them and guide the teachers.

3. At the national level, too, there should be an ideal institution capable of working for the improvement of education. At present, the NCERT is performing this function, but it is necessary to make its efforts more fruitful in a shorter time frame.

4. At the district level, there should be strong organisation under the direction for the district education officer, and the principals of all training colleges in the district should offer him their co-operation.
5. In the states, too, there is the need to establish such institutions as—state secondary education board, teacher training board, text-books improvement centre, curriculum research institute, vocational guidance institute, etc.

Supervision

Although various suggestions have been given for making supervision and guidance of schools more effective and these include formation and implementation of institutional plans, reorganisation of the department of education, adoption of the school complex scheme, introduction of panel inspection, etc., it is equally important to raise the standard of inspection through the proper training of the inspecting staff. For this, the first step is to increase the number of inspectors, because at present, each inspecting officer has the responsibility for inspecting the working of between 22 and 246 institutions, (an average of 51), and between 94 and 1091 teachers (an average of 197). The second step is the appointment of specialist officials, in addition to the general inspection staff, and the former should be capable not only of evaluating the teacher's teaching work but also of guiding him. These specialists should be of two kinds-one, those who pay complete attention to the teaching in specific subjects, such as mathematics, science, English, etc., two, those who possess specific qualifications in such fields as programming, physical education, improvement of examination system, construction of courses, etc. These specialists should be entrusted, not merely with the routine inspection of schools, but with the task of providing in-service training and guidance. Initially, specialist inspectors should be appointed for particular subjects in some selected districts.

Implementation

The fourth programme for the improvement in administration is the modification and modernisation of the department's method of working, which, at present, is in a deplorable state. For this purpose, the measures outlined below should be adopted :

1. The department of education in each state should have a wing for the study of organisation and working, and it should offer its suggestions for administrative reforms from time to time.

2. The National College, whose establishment has been recommended by the Kothari Commission, should provide opportunities for research into educational administration. In addition it should study the following subjects and offer its suggestions and rules pertaining to admission to educational institutions of particular classes, provision of financial grants to institutions, selection of teachers, evaluation of teaching work, determining the internal and external techniques of evaluation, adoption of a convenient method for payment of teachers salaries, preparation of text-books and their acceptance, and analysis of the work of official concerned with inspection and supervision.

3. Excessive and unnecessary staff should not be appointed, but at the same time, care should be taken to see that important officials do not waste their time and energies in routine and minor works.

4. Delays in work and inconveniences are occasioned by an irrational division of authority. Hence, as far as possible, more and more administrative and

financial responsibility should be shifted to district level officials. The directorate of education should concern itself mainly with co-ordinating their efforts, formulating policies, and ascertaining whether the authority delegated to them is being properly utilised or not.

5. In the annual conferences of educational administrators of various levels, information about departmental policies and programmes should be given, but in addition, they should also be made aware of the changes introduced. Their views on these changes should be invited and discussions initiated.

In this context, it is to be noted that improvements in departmental working require officials with open minds and hearts. When the organisation suggested above it introduced, it is hoped that these administrators will be able to develop the right attitudes.

Factors at Work

The fifth step towards the improvement in administration lies in introducing flexibility and dynamism in administration. The problems of India's education are very complex and the diversities and variety in the country's economic and social conditions have obviated the possibility of finding a single solution for them all, under all conditions. Even this diversity can be converted into a virtue if the method of working is dynamic and flexible. What will happen in such a situation is that varied experiments will be carried out in different situations and contexts, and with their help, solutions will be found quickly and inexpensively. This important principle can best be illustrated through some examples.

1. Under the present educational system, all the colleges and schools in the state have a common curriculum, and whatever changes are introduced usually

produce destructive results in certain plans. The reason for this is that those who formulate the curriculum invariably keep their vision fixed upon the weaker and backward students. In consequence, the brilliant students and enthusiastic institutions are never benefited. Besides, the rigid curriculum makes it impossible to exploit the institutional advantages that some institutions may have over others. Hence, it is essential that, in a state, more than one, or at least two curricula—one generalist and the other specialised, must be introduced.

2. No less important is flexibility and variability in the methods of teaching and evaluation. The existing fixed methods, a fixed curriculum and a definite system of education may satisfy the average teacher and the average student. But teachers with creative minds, if prevented from working outside the guidelines fixed by the department, will be completely stultified.

3. The second rigid constraint in the existing system is that the child makes his choice of subjects in class 9, at the age of 14, and then remain tied to this choice for the future. This kind of responsibility, thrust upon the immature child, is as harmful in the long run as the institution of child marriage proved to be. Besides, deciding upon groups of subjects is also counter productive.

4. Efforts at making secondary education development oriented and reducing the enrolment in research at the university level have both failed. Hence, a plan should be prepared in which the curricula for the first degree synthesizes a number of vocational studies. Later on, specialised education in those vocations should be provided, to the extent of

allowing the candidate to obtain his Ph.D. degree in the subject, if he so wishes.

5. The current fashion is to give financial grants upon certain fixed principles to all educational institutions, with the result that the superior as well as the inferior institution obtain under the same rules and conditions. This policy of uniformity should be modified so as to make provisions or additional grants to the better and more progressive institutions.
6. There should be a practical and flexible approach towards the medium of education. So long as regional languages remain incapable of shouldering the burden. English should be retained as the medium of education, in order to maintain standards.
7. There should be flexibility even in the sphere of education. At present, an excessive expansion in secondary and higher secondary education in certain regions has led to increased unemployment while on the other hand in some regions, these levels of education have been introduced quite recently. In the future, expansion of education should be limited only to the underdeveloped regions only.

It is of course true that it is as difficult and problematic to implement a flexible and dynamic method of education as it is easy and convenient to implement a rigid and uniform system of education. But, in modern society, we just cannot make progress without a flexible and dynamic system. In fact, we must now grant freedom to every student, every teacher and every institution.

❐

15

National Education Policy

A nation is said to be strong and united when devisive forces causing distintegration are totally absent in it. A nation is socially integrated when all its members enjoy a sense of equality of opportunities in political, economic and social spheres of activity and when they have mutual understanding of respect for each other's ways of life. A country is said to be nationally integrated when its people rise above sectional loyalties and identify themselves with the nation as a whole and have faith in the nation's future.

Gravity of the Problem. The attainment of social and national integration as one of the objectives of the national system of education is a challenging problem. For a country like ours, it is difficult to achieve this objective because there is already a wide gulf between the rich and the poor, the urban and the rural, the elite and the masses. Besides, people are bound by local, regional, linguistic, religious and other sectional ties. Old traditions and values are rapidly disappearing. Education is promoting devisive tendencies. The schools for the rich and the poor are segregated. There is a lack of national consciousness everywhere. Communal riots, corruption, strikes, lawlessness, disregard for public property are some of the symptoms of social distingration.

Steps Suggested. The Education Commission (1964-66) suggested certain steps to create a strong and united country to make people conscious of what 'India' is and to create an integrated society. This could be done by the introduction of the common school, by making social and national service an integral part of education at all stages, by adopting a proper language policy and by promoting national consciousness.

1. The Common School System. The educational system as it exists even today is undemocratic and harmful for national unity and social solidarity. It is undemocratic because under this system good education is not available to all children. The children of the masses are sent to schools managed by the government or by the local authorities. The schools charge either no fees or normal fees. They provide sub-standard or poor quality education. The children of the privileged class are sent to the private, fee-charging, better schools. The present system of education is harmful for the country not only because 'the identification and development of the total national pool of ability is greatly hampered', but also because it weakens social cohesion.

The common school system of public education has been suggested by the Commission as a powerful instrument for achieving social and national integration, because the schools under this system would be open to 'all children, irrespective of caste, creed, community, religion, economic conditions or social status'. As these schools would maintain adequate standards the rich people will tend to send their children to them and as they will not charge any fees, they would meet the needs of average parents too.

2. Social and National Service as an Integral Part of Education. The Commission suggested that programmes of social and national service should be incorporated in the education of children at all stages. The programmes should run together with academic studies in schools and colleges and start from the upper primary stage (V-VII) and continue up to the university. Social service may take the form of participation in community living on the school or college campus or in programmes of community development. Every school and college should try to develop a rich community life for its students and should provide adequate opportunities to them to participate in it; for example, much of the work done by hired labour or menial servants can be done by students themselves. Money so saved may be used for providing amenities to them. Programmes of community service may also be integrated in school and college education. At the higher primary stage students may be encouraged to serve the community in a number of ways. At the secondary stage suitable forms of service to the community may be sought after. At the college level participation in Labour and Social Welfare camps or the N.C.C. may be made obligatory and programmes of community development may be developed agreeing with the available resources, age and competence of students.

Social and national service so organised and made obligatory for all students at all stages would certainly lead to a decrease in the social distance between the educated and the uneducated, the intelligentsia and the masses. It will also help up in evolving a united nation.

3. Evolving a Language Policy for National and Social Integration. The Emotional Integration Committee regarded the use of regional languages from the primary to the college level as media of education, 'a matter of profound importance for national integration'. The National Integration Council (1962) spoke in support of the same view. The Education Commission (1964-66) also agreed with these observations. The Commission recommended that regional languages should be made media of instruction at all levels, that Hindi should be so developed that it becomes the link language of the people in the shortest time possible, and English may continue as the link language of the intellectual people or it may function as library language at all stages of education. The language question which had been very 'complex and intractable' so far has been solved by the Commission to the satisfaction of all.

4. Promoting National Consciousness. The schools under the English regime taught loyalty to the English people by giving instruction to our students in their literature, history and culture. Love for the motherland was never developed before 1937. It was the struggle for Independence between 1900 and 1947 that made people nationally conscious. The development of national consciousness was effected outside the school walls.

After the attainment of Independence in 1947, the people began to forget 'India'. Sectional loyalties grew up. Schools remained sleeping. The unfortunate international conflicts—the Chinese invasion of 1962, the two recent aggressions by Pakistan—did something to unite us. But such happenings could never be regarded as a right solution. Can education be not used as an effective tool for promoting national consciousness? Schools and colleges in other countries have done so.

The Education Commission believed firmly in the efficacy of formal education for promoting national spirit in the educand. It suggested that the Indian youth could be made to understand his cultural heritage by a well-organised instruction in Indian languages, literature, history and philosophy, and that he could be helped to instil faith in the future of the nation through a systematic course in civics and politics and political economy.

Circumstances to Setup the Education Commission (1964-66)

A Need for Social Change after Independence. Education, all the world over, has been used as a powerful tool of social, economic and political change. The political upheaval that took place in our country in the beginning of the century brought in its train a set of changes in the life of the nation. A need began to be felt to bring about a multiphased revolution within the shortest possible period. The whole government machinery was set in motion for making an effort at economic growth, social change and cultural advancement. As the government was convinced that education is the key to national prosperity and welfare, an all-out attempt was made to transform the education system.

A Need for Evolving a National System of Education. In spite of much valuable thinking and considerable implementation of educational ideas during the 15 years that followed the attainment of Independence, the nation could not develop a system of education which could meet the needs of the newly born democratic state. The Government of India expressed its grave concern at the state of affairs in 1964 in the following words, "While some advances have been made in (certain) directions, the education system has not generally evolved in accordance with the needs of the times, and a wide and distressing gulf continues to persist between thought and action in several sectors of this crucial field of national activity." The views expressed by eminent educationists to evolve a national system of education or the recommendations made by Committees and Commissions (especially appointed ever since the achievement of Independence) were either ignored or partially implemented. For example, the Higher Secondary (three years) pattern was not given a fair trial in most of the states. The scheme of basic education could not achieve desired success. The multipurpose scheme of diversified courses have to meet the same fate.

During the three Plan periods education at all levels had expanded tremendously. Yet people were not happy about a number of educational aspects: for example, the nation was not yet able to provide free and compulsory education for all children of 14 + ; nor could it solve the problem of educated unemployment throught diversification of courses nor could it produce an adequate supply of manpower in many sectors of economic life nor could it raise the status of the teaching community. Quantitative expansion of education did take place, but qualitative improvements suffered.

Realising the importance of education in the bringing about of the desired economic and social development, the Government of India in 1964 considered the urgency of surveying and examining the entire field of education. Problems of educational reconstruction had been reviewed by a number of Committees and Commissions which attempted to solve difficulties faced in specific areas only. For example, the University Education Commission (1948-49) and the Secondary Education Commission (1952-53) surveyed the fields of university and school education respectively. Towards the end of the Third Five Year Plan, a need began to be felt to make a review of the present education system so comprehensive that it may cover the entire field.

A Need for Improving Quality of Education. The need for appointing a fresh Education Commission in 1964 arose out of a grave concern for the improvement of quality of education. The Government wanted an expert advice on the evolution of the much desired national system of education and on the formation of 'general principles and policies for the development of education at all stages and in all aspects.' The Resolution of the Government of India in 1964 said, "It is desirable to survey the entire field of educational development as the various parts of the educational system strongly interact with and influence one another. It is not possible to have progressive and strong universities without efficient secondary school and the quality of these schools is determined by the functioning of elementary schools. What is needed, therefore, is a synoptic survey and an imaginative look at education considered as a whole and not fragmented into parts and stages. In the past several commissions and committees have examined limited sectors and specific aspects of education. It is now proposed to have a comprehensive review of the entire educational system."

NATIONAL POLICY OF EDUCATION, 1986

On April 20, 1986 a new Educational Policy was placed before the Indian Parliament for consideration and approval. The following objectives of education were particularly emphasized in this policy:

1. Vocationalization of Education. Particularly, at the secondary stage of education the curriculum should be job-oriented.
2. To encourage the governmental and non-governmental efforts for wiping out illiteracy and to emphasize the necessity of adult education, formal education, farmers' education and 'open' schools.
3. To awaken the people about the various scientific and technological developments and to make the students at the various stages of education aware of the same in order that they may utilize them in their future life.

Onwards we shall look into some basic details of this new policy:

1. National Forum of Education. At least 75 per cent of the curriculum should be identical for all the States. The remaining 25 per cent may be related to the particular local conditions of a State. The purpose of incorporation this basic feature is to acquaint all the citizens of the country with their basic rights and duties, history of the freedom struggle, the common cultural heritage and national identity.

2. Delinking Degree for any Service. If the compulsoriness of a degree for securing a job is done away with, many youths will automatically refrain from obtaining higher education. Thus crowding of aspirants for admissions to colleges and universities will be reduced. In fact, a degree should not be considered as a pre-requisite for a job which has not direct relationship with it. In many foreign developed countries a degree is not considered as a condition for obtaining a job. According to the 1991 Census Report a degree is considered in our country as a requisite for securing a service. At the T.V. centres for the Chaupal or Krishi Darshan Programmes, B.Sc. (Agr.) has been made as compulsory for a person conducting them. Similarly, in our country a degree has been made compulsory for a job. In fact, many students of our colleges and universities have absolutely no interest in their studies.

3. Emphasis on Learning. The teacher must not harbour the notion that the child learns through his teaching alone. In fact, the child learns many more things by himself. Therefore, the teacher must not emphasize only by teaching procedures in the class-room. Essentially, he should also try to create such an environment in the class and school in general that the children may learn many things through their own creativeness. The prescribed curriculum for children do not contain the latest informations of the concerned subject. Generally, they are four or five years old. So they are not very useful, because they contain incomplete informations. Therefore the teacher must inspire the students to learn things on their own as far as possible. The mental development of children should be so guided that they make understand the utility of knowledge themselves. The Education Policy of 1986 has particularly emphasised this point.

4. Education for the Weaker Section of the Society. The education of scheduled castes, scheduled tribes, handicapped and girls has been greatly emphasised because in the interest of national progress, their development has been considered necessary. Hence, reservation for such persons has been recommended in various types of educational institution.

5. Vocationalization of Education. Vocationalization of education has been particularly been emphasised in this new education policy. As far as possible, education should be given in a natural environment. The child must acquire some skill in some area of his interest. This is necessary for a happy life in future. With this end in view this new education policy has advocated for inclusion of scientific and technical subjects in the curriculum. It has been specifically stated in the policy that in the tenth class not more than 50 per cent students should opt for literacy subjects and the rest should be encouraged to study vocational courses of various types according to their interests. This kind of vocationalization of education will minimise the unemployment problem, because then the educated person will not depend on some service alone and may utilize his acquired skill for earning his bread.

6. Emphasis on Reforms in Examination System. It has been suggested in this new policy that 'grade' should be given in examination in place of 'division'. In the current system of examination the student scoring between 45 to 48 per cent of marks is placed in the second class and those sixty or above are placed in the first class. In this situation the students getting within the range of 44 and 47 and also only 59 think that they have lost their higher division by one mark only. This feature develops a kind of frustration and anguish in them. In order to do away with this situation, this new policy has suggested giving of "grades" and not "class" or "division". According to this new policy those coming within the range of 40 to 50 or of 45 to 55 will be given "B" or "C" grade. A determination of assigning "B" or "C" grade will depend upon the nature of achievements of all the students taking up an examination. Suppose in a certain difficult test no student scores more than 45 per cent, then it is just possible that it may be considered desirable that those scoring 45 per cent or above may be given "A" grade and those getting 40 may be grouped under "B" and those 35 may be assigned "C" grade. Thus assigning of "grades" will depend upon the nature of a test and how all the students as a whole show performance on the same. Periodical tests have also been recommended in this new policy, because the determination of merit of a student on the basis of only one examination has not been considered as just. Similarly, appointment of external examiners, too, has been considered as undesirable. Thus the teachers have been made solely responsible for evaluating the merits of his students. It has been felt that this method will increase the importance of teachers and marks of indiscipline in students will also be gradually minimised.

7. Importance of Moral Values. The importance of moral values has been recognised by this new policy. The development of healthy moral values in an individual will help him to depend upon his own efforts and not on his self-imposed destiny. Education is a tool for bringing in desirable changes in a society. Therefore importance of moal values in life should be pointed out wherever possible in teaching. This method of teaching moral values will be more helpful to students.

8. Ever-Continual Primary School. According to this new education policy each primary school will have at least a two-room-building with at least two teachers. Of these two teachers, one will be a lady. Each primary school will function throughout the twelve months a year. Thus all the young children in an area will be receiving primary education.

9. All India Educational Service. In order to tone up educational administration, this policy has emphasised the necessity of starting an All India Education Service cadre. Under this scheme any education officer may be transferred any where in the country. It has been felt that this kind of transfer will weaken the undesirable bond of regionalism and will bring dynamism in the educational administration. The policy of transfer will dissuade the education officers from coming into the pressure of politicians in the sphere of their work and as a result they will be more honest in the performance of their duties.

10. Modernization of Education. Computerisation has been suggested in this policy. This method will be employed in the expansion of literacy. The utility of correspondence courses, T.V., Radio and Satellite, and Video-cassetts has been accepted for education in this policy.

11. Importance of Sports and Games. In this new policy importance of sports and games has been recognised because participation in them will maintain the health of children. With this end in view forming of active committees of sports and games has been particularly emphasised. Framing of curriculum of small sports and games has also been suggested.

12. Right Persons Alone to be Teachers. This education policy has considered the training of teacher as very important for raising the falling standard of education. Hence, some very useful suggestions have been given for improving the condition of teachers. According to this policy the teachers of a certain cadre should enjoy identical scale of salaries and all of them should be given residential facilitis. The society should be well awakened for giving due respects to teachers. Refresher course for teachers after every five years period has been considered necessary in order to acquaint them with the latest developed teachnique of teaching.

13. Establishing Navodaya Schools. Students in these schools will be admitted to class VI on the basis of an admission test. In the admission process pre-determined ratio for boys and girls of both urban and rural areas will be observed. In admission to these schools no financial criterion will be observed. All these boy and girl students will have to reside in the respective associated hostels after being admitted to the Navodaya schools. Such students will be given free boarding and lodging and free education. Twenty per cent of the students after passing 8th class in a Navodaya school will be transferred for education to other States with a view to promote national integration.

14. Open University. In this policy starting of Open Universities has been emphasised. These universities are meant for those persons who have not been able to obain higher education, but are desirous of receiving the same in order to better their prospects. The necessity of open universities has been recognised also for expansion of higher education. In an open university any person may obtain higher education according to his own speed. A certain examination may be passed in parts in an open university.

15. New Educational Institutions. In the education policy of 1986, it has been recommended that "District Institute of Education and Training" and "District of Education" should be established in the various states of the country. These institutions will survey the educational needs of people of various areas separately and will inform the concerned education officers about the same from time to time. The constitution of a national institute has also been proposed with a view to raise the standard of education. The main purpose of the new policy has been to prepare such citizens for the coming twenty-first century who may be responsive to their basic duties in consonance with human values and democratic ideals.

16. Protection of Environment Necessary. Protection of environment has been emphasised in the new policy of 1986.

The students and teachers will be urged to protect rivers, lakes, hills, mountains, forests, and pasture lands. They will also see that the existing mills and factories do not pollute the surrounding environments.

17. Women Education. According to this policy the standard of education of women should be raised. In vocational and technical education, women will be assigned their proper place in order to equate them with men as far as possible. An attempt will also be made to minimise the difference existing in the curriculum meant for women and men.

18. Preservation of Own Culture. There appears to be a wide gulf between the modern formal education and our cultural traditions. This new education policy wants to bridge this gulf, because the scientific and technical developments have to be associated with our proud history and culture. Our system of education should be related with our Fine Arts, Architecture and Oriental Studies. Hence we shall have to pay particular attention on organisation of museums, folk arts and literature. This policy urges us to do the needful in these directions. Modern education has led many of our youths to drug-addiction and it has not taught many of them how to be respectful to teachers and other elders in the society. As a result, deplorable marks of indiscipline in these usually stare at us.

19. Adult Education. A literacy programme will be organised for making illiterate persons literate within the age group of 15 and 35. For this purpose Continuing Education Centres will be established in rural areas. It will be a duty of a Project Officer to spread literacy amongst labourers. Distance education will be given through Radio, T.V. and films. These media will be utilized for vocational programmes as well.

20. Operation Black Board. In this new policy the term "Operation Black Board" has been used for conveying the ideas that minimum facilities will be provided to a primary school. These minimum facilities will include at least two rooms, some necessary charts and maps, a black-board, Tatpatti (about one metre wide and 10 metre long pieces of carpet) for seating children and other essential material equipments. In the beginning at least two teachers will be appointed for each primary school. Afterwards more teachers may be appointed as new classes are added. In the "Operation Black Board" the co-operation of voluntary organisations, local bodies and desirous persons will be enlisted. At first-some building will be provided to a primary school if it does not have any.

Philosophy of New Policy

1. New Acculturating Role of Education. One of the most important contributions of New Policy of Education is that it has provided a comprehensive educational philosophy covering the new acculturating role of education by way of refining sensitiveness, building scientific temper and cultivating independence of mind and spirit.

2. Natural Perspective. Manpower planning and its educational investment has brought in a national perspective to our development needs. A unifying policy in the development of human resources provides a social dimension to an area of personal perception. The pooling of resources in the area of personnel and research at the national level with the provision for interregional mobility with equal access for every Indian of requisite merit is a most welcome and timely policy statement.

3. Equalisation. The special emphasis laid on the removal of disparities and equalization of opportunity by attending to the specific needs of different groups of distressed people including women, scheduled castes, minorities and the handicapped, should enhance the sense of social responsibility and a fair distribution on justice to all concerned.

4. Efficiency. The policy determination to promote efficiency and effectiveness at all levels (though easier said that done) brings in new dimension in the performance of teachers, students, administrators, Government officials and institutions.

5. Universalisation. The universalisation of education upto a given level with access of education of a comparable quality is another positive aspect of the policy.

6. Cultural Perspective. Another special feature of the policy is the concept of providing a cultural perspective in the formal system of education.

7. Beneficial. The realisation of education needs to be managed in an atmosphere of ultmost intellectual rigour, seriousness of purposes with adequate freedom for innovation and creativity should bear beneficial fruits.

8. Value Education. The focus on value education and work experience as an integral part of the learning process will enable us to uphold human values necessary for raising the quality of life for all. The document speaks about combating certain negative values and promoting positive ones from our heritage. It mentions social, ethical and moral values which have to be cultivated.

The Essence and Role of Education

The policy envisaged the role of education as follows—

1. Education is fundamental to our all-round development, material and spiritual.
2. Education is the highway to derive the maximum benefit from the areas already created by the economic and technical development and a means to ensure that the funds must reach all sections.
3. Education has an acculturating role. It refines sensitivity and perceptions that contribute to national

cohesion, a scientific temper and independence of mind and spirit.

4. Education should be an effective instrument of reducing rural-urban disparities.
5. Education needs to be planned meticulously and developed with great sensitivity so as to make the best use of the human being who is a positive asset and precious national resources.
6. Spread of literacy and education among women in the largest single factor in bringing down the growth of population in India.
7. Education must prevent the erosion of long-cherished values.
8. Education should imbibe the coming generations with a strong commitment of human values and to social justice.
9. Education should assist in the realisation of goals of secularism, socialism and professional ethics.
10. Education develops manpower of different level of the economy.
11. Education should develop the activity of the coming generation to internalize new ideas constantly and creatively.
12. Education is unique investment in the present and the future.

Features of National System of Education Envisaged by NPE, 1986.

The National Policy on Education, 1986 has envisaged the following main features of the National Systems of Education:

1. Based on Constitutional Principles. It derives its inspiration from the ideals and values of democracy, secularism and socialism enshrined in our Constitution.

2. Access of Education. It implies that upto a given level all students, irrespective of caste, creed, location, sex, have access to education of a comparable quality. To achieve this, the Government will initiate appropriate funded programmes. Effective measures will be taken in the direction of the Common School recommended in the 1968 policy.

3. Minimum Levels of Learning. Minimum levels of learning will be laid down for each stage of education. Steps will also be taken to foster students an understanding of the diverse cultural and social systems of the people living in different parts of the country.

4. Education for International Understanding. India has always worked for peace and understanding between nations, treating the whole world as one family. True to this hoary, tradition, education has to strengthen this world view and motivate the younger generations for international co-operation and peaceful co-existence. This aspect cannot be neglected.

5. Common Educational Structure. It envisages of common educational structure. The 10+2+3 structure has now been accepted in all parts of the country. Regarding the further break-up of the first 10 years efforts will be made to move towards an elementary system comprising five years of primary education and three years of upper primary, followed by two years of High School.

6. National Curricular Framework with a Common Core. It will be based on a national curricular framework which contains a common core along with other components that are flexible. The common core will include the history of

India's freedom movement, the constitutional obligations and other contents essential to nurture national identity. These elements cut across subject areas and will be designed to promote values such as India's common cultural heritage, egalitarianism, democracy and secularism, equality of the sexes, protection of the environment, removal of social barriers, observance of the small family norms and inculcation of the scientific temper. All educational programmes will be carried on in strict conformity with secular values.

7. Universal Character of Higher Education. In higher education in general and technical education in particular, steps will be taken to facilitate inter-regional mobility by providing equal access to every Indian of requisite merit, regardless of his origins. The universal character of universities and other institutions of higher education is to be understood.

8. Promotion of Languages. Besides the promotion of the link language, programmes will also be launched to increase substantially the translation of books form glossaries. The young will be encouraged to undertake the rediscovery of India each in his own image and perception.

9. Priorities in Educational Reform. The Nation as a whole will assume the responsibility of providing resource support for implementing programmes of educational transformation, reducing disparities, universalisation of elementary education, adult literacy, scientific and technical research, etc.

10. Equality of Opportunity in Education. To promote equality it will be necessary to provide for equal opportunity to all not only in access, but also in the conditions for success. Besides, awareness of the inherent equality of all will be created through the core curriculum. The purpose is to remove prejudices and complexes transmitted through the social environment and accident of birth.

11. Open and Distance Learning. Life-long education is a cherished goal of the education process. This presupposes universal literacy. Opportunities will be provided to the youth, house-wives, agricultural and industrial workers and professionals to continue the education of the choice, and the pace suited to them. The further thrust will be in the direction of open and distance learning.

12. Strengthening of National Institutions. National institutions which will be strengthened to play an important role in giving shape to the National System of Education, are the University Grants Commission. The All India Council of Technical Education, the Indian Council of Agricultural Research and the Indian Medical Council. Integrated Planning will be instituted among all these bodies so as to establish functional linkages and reinforce programmes of research and post graduate education. These, together with the National Council of Education Research and Training, the National Institute of Educational Planning and Administration and the International Institute of Science and Technology Education will be involved in implementing the Education Policy.

EIGHT BOLD STEPS OF NPE, 1986

1. National System of Education. National system of education to provide access to education of a comparable quality to all students, to have a common educational structure with national curricular framework containing a common core.

2. Navodaya Schools. Pace setting Navodaya Schools to be started which will be residential and free of charge.

3. Vocational Targets. Vocational courses to cover 10 per cent of higher secondary students by 1990 and 25 per cent by 1955.

4. Performance and Accountability. To ensure that all teachers should teach and all students study.

5. Delinking Degree from Jobs. Beginning to be made in delinking degrees from jobs in selected areas.

6. The Management of Education. Evolving a strategy of decentralization and the creation of a spirit of autonomy for educational institutions.

7. Indian Education Service. Constitution of this Service is likely to bring a national perspective in education.

8. Raising Resources. Resources to be raised through:

(i) Asking beneficiary communities to maintain school buildings,

(ii) Raising fees at the higher levels of education, and

(iii) Levying cess or charge on the user agencies.

Missing Links and Limitations

1. Confined to Privileged. A lion's share of the benefit of education is cornered by about six per cent of students who have been fortunate to join colleges. It is this privileged section which corners 99 per cent of Government jobs. Educational expenditure has become a mechanism of transferring resources from rural sector to urban sector or in other words from poor to the rich.

2. Neglect of Neighbourhood Concepts. The New Education Policy has completely ignored the 'neighbourhood' concept of school system advocated by the Kothari Commission. It is interesting to note that the Kothari Commission considered that the 'neighbourhood School' was a step towards eliminating the segregation that now takes place between the schools for the poor and the underprivileged classes and those for the rich and the privileged one.

3. Need of Basic Education. The Education Policy does not refer to Basic Education although it has an important place in the ideology of freedom struggle and procedures were finalised as long back as 1937.

4. No Reference to Working Days. The New Education Policy should have recommended increased number of working days in educational institutions. There should be about 300 working days instead of about 200 at present.

5. Wrong Basics of Reservation. The New Education Policy should have suggested reservation not on the basics of merit but on the basics of economic conditions.

6. No Check on Nursery Schools. The New Education Policy has not mentioned concrete steps to curb the mushroom growth of nursery schools charging high fees and meant only for the rich.

7. Lack of Teachers and Equipments. The emphasis on teaching and learning through discovery has little meaning as the nation has thousands of schools without adequate teachers and equipment.

8. No Check on Minority Institutions. Some suitable checks on the working of the schools run by the minority communities should have been proposed so as to prevent them from exploiting the staff working in these institutions.

9. No Research Basis. There is practically no proposal in the documents which is based on authentic research.

10. No Supervision. The New Education Policy does not include specific measures for supervising and monitoring Government and Central schools properly. There is an urgent need to ensure that, 'All teachers should teach and all students study'.

11. No Check on Public Schools. The New Education Policy has, by and large, evaded the issue of the 'loot' by so-called public schools which take money only and do not give good education.

12. No Fixed Target. It is very unfortunate that no target has been fixed in different areas of reforms.

13. Multiplication of Authorities. Setting up State Advisory Boards of Education, District Institutes of Education and District Boards of Education is not likely to serve any useful purpose. Already there is multiplicity of authorities in the field of education.

14. Lack of Funds. There is very little hope of obtaining community funds for educational purposes as there is a growing tendency on the part of the rich members of the community to contribute liberally to political parties due to obvious reasons. People, in general, are not motivated to donate funds for welfare services.

Revised Policy Formulations, May 1992

The National Policy of Education (NPE), 1986 is a landmark in educational development of the country. A review of the NPE, 1986 was conducted during 1990-92. The Central Advisory Board of Education (CABE) in its 47th meeting held on May 5-6, 1992 considered the report of the CABE Committee on policy set-up to make an in-depth study of the report of the Committee for review of NPE, 1986. While broadly endorsing the policy, it recommended certain modifications in the light of the developments during the last few years and the experience gained in the implementation of the policy. The revised policy formulations containing these modifications recommended by the CABE were tabled in the Parliament on May 7, 1992.

Following the adoption of the revised policy formulations in May 1992, a revised POA was prepared. The POA 1992 was tabled in the Parliament on August 19, 1992.

Universalisation of elementary education, equalization of educational opportunities, women's education and development, vocationalisation of school education, consolidation of higher education, modernization of technical education, improvement of quality content and process of education at all levels continue to be the themes of national endeavour in the field of education.

Committee for Girls Education and Public Corporation 1963-65.

Committee for Girls' Education and Public Co-operation (1963-65). At its meeting held in April, 1963 the National Council for Women's Education endorsed the suggestion made by the Union Education Minister that a small committee be appointed to look into the causes for lack of public support, particularly in rural areas, for girls' education and to enlist public co-operation. The Chairman of the National Council for Women's Education accordingly appointed in May 1963, a Committee with M. Bhaktavatsalam, Chief Minister, Madras as Chairman the Committee in this field. The Committee submitted its report in 1964 and the report was published in 1965.

Recommendations

It is only through a willing, educated and informed public that any progress can be made at all. Not only is the need urgent, but the ground is also ready for a comprehensive programme for mobilizing public co-operation to promote girls' education and giving it constructive channels for expression. It is essential that official action and the programme based on public initiative must move forward in close foremen. There has to be a sense of partnership and shared responsibility between official and voluntary agencies. There is also the need for a systematic and sustained programme with an adequate organisation for mobilizing community efforts.

1. Public Co-operation. Direct co-operation of the public should be encouraged in the following fields :

(i) Establishing private schools;

(ii) Putting up of schools buildings;

(iii) Contributing volunatary labour for construction of school buildings;

(iv) Helping in providing suitable accommodation for teachers and students, particularly in the rural areas;

(v) Helping in the maintenances of school buildings;

(vi) Popularising co-education at the primary stage;

(vii) Creating public opinion in favour of the teaching profession and to give greater respect to the teacher in the community;

(viii) Initiating action and participating in educative propaganda to break down traditional prejudices against girls' education;

(ix) Setting up and organizing school betterment committees, improvement conferences;

(x) Undertaking necessary propaganda to make the profession of teaching for women popular;

(xi) Encouraging married women to take up at least part-time teaching in village schools and to work as school mothers;

(xii) Supplying mid-day meals;

(xiii) Supplying free text-books and writing materials to needy children; and

(xiii) Supplying uniforms to poor and needy children.

2. The State Council for Women's Education. These are the most suitable agencies for providing the organisation and leadership for mobilizing community effort. They should function as a part of the network of which the district Councils at the district level, and the Mahila Mandals and similar voluntary bodies at the town and village levels would be strong and active links. These agencies should look upon mobilising of community effort and educating public opinion to promote girls' education as their main and primary responsibility. They should aim at building up in villages and towns' teams of volunary workers, men and women, who are willing to devote themselves to this cause and work actively for its promotion.

3. State's Responsibility. The State should educate public opinion in favour of girls' education through:

(i) School improvement conferences;

(ii) Seminars;

(iii) Assisting voluntary, welfare and other organisations, private individuals and associations engaged in the field of education of girls and women;

(iv) Radio talks, audio-visual aids and distribution of informative pamphlets;

(v) Enrolment drives, generally in June and special additional drives for girls' education during Dussehra.

4. State Help. The State should continue to help in an abundant measure in providing necessary schooling facilities in all the areas and in the habitations, however, so that the local population can make use of them.

5. School Improvement Conferences. These should be arranged widely throughout the State and particularly in the less advanced States in order to encourage people to contribute to educational awakening and advancement.

6. Pre-Primary Schools. It is necessary that in rural areas paricularly, pre-primary schools should be attached to primary schools so that children get accustomed to schooling even at the tender age.

7. More Attractive. School work should be made more attractive and should present education in terms more acceptable to pupils.

8. Reform and Inspection. The existing functional deficiencies of schools should be remedied by replacing buildings which are totally inadequate to modern educational needs. There should be periodical inspection of school buildings and hostels so as to ensure their structural soundness and suitable sanitary facilities.

9. Recruitment of Women Teachers. Concerted efforts have to be made to recruit as many women teachers as possible. Women are by general consent the best teachers forth primary classes in all schools. It should be the aim of all states to appoint women teachers in primary schools and a greater number of women teachers in mixed schools. A school staffed by women will inspire greater confidence in the parents and make them willing to send their children to mixed institutions.

(i) Conditions of Recruitment. The basis of recruitment of women teachers should be widened and their conditions of work should be made more attractive. Financial incentives like special allowances for hilly, isolated or any other specific backward rural areas should be given to teachers. Each State may specify areas where such allowances would be available.

(ii) Recruitment Age Limit. In order to attract more women teachers the age limit for the unmarried and

married women teachers should be relaxed in the case of those working in village schools. The service conditions of such married women who do part-time teaching work should be made more attractive.

(iii) ***Married Women Teachers.*** Attempt should be made to bring back to the teaching profession married women who have left it in recent years and to bring women from other occupations to supplement the teaching staff.

(iv) ***Posting.*** As far as possible women teachers should be posted in or near their own villages.

(v) ***Condensed Courses.*** Condensed courses should be organised on a large scale foretold, women particularly from rural areas so that they could take up teaching jobs in the villages.

(vi) ***Training Schools.*** Training schools with hostels need to be located in the rural centres and near 'different' areas where girls from the villages are trained and sent back to work in their own or neighbouring villages.

(vii) ***Special Attention.*** Special drives should be organised to as the best form of social service needed for the upliftment of the villages.

(viii) ***Pay Scale.*** The pay scales of all teachers should be improved and the teachers should be paid an economic wage, so that they may be retained in the profession.

(ix) ***Training.*** During selection of trainees for training schools and colleges, special preference should be given to women from rural areas seeking admission.

(x) ***Sufficient Facilities.*** The training facilities available in each State should be of such a magnitude that the annual output of trained teachers would be equal to the demand for additional teachers.

(xi) ***Hostels.*** The absence of hostel facilities as also the slow progress in the construction of those that have been undertaken, have affected the hostel. The construction of hostels should be included as one of the priority objectives in the Plans of the States and necessary financial assistance for the construction of hostels and maintenance stipends be made available more liberally to local authorities and voluntary organisations working in the field of education of girls and women.

(xii) ***Lodging.*** It is only by providing women teachers with quarters near the schools that we can attract many educated women to the teaching profession.

(xiii) ***Inspection.*** The inspecting staff should be adequate and strong if improvement into be secured and waste reduced. A separate women inspectorate will help to bring in more girls to school.

10. Building and Equipment. Local bodies should be made responsible for the provision of school buildings, equipments, playing fields and the like and observance of the educational code in the State.

11. Social Education. In the field of social education, a determined effort should be made to increase the number of literacy classes for women in rural areas and to carry out intensive campaigns for the spread of literacy amongst women. Activities in this field should be administered by the education departments of the State Government.

12. Central Assistance. Such Central assistance should be—

(a) At the elementary stage for:

- (i) preparation and employment of women teachers;
- (ii) grant of free books, writing material and clothing to girls; and
- (iii) twin quarters for women teachers.

(b) At the secondary stage for:

- (i) provision of separate schools for girls;
- (ii) hostels;
- (iii) grant of free books, writing materials and clothing to girls; and
- (iv) preparation and appointment of women teachers in increasing numbers.

13. Curriculum. While the curriculum can be the same for both boys and girls at the primary and middle stages, provision should be made for offering of electives comprising subjects which would be of special interest to girls and which would help them later in their fields of activity.

14. Seasonal Adjustment. Changing of school hours and school holidays to seasonal requirements has been found in some places to be a helpful concession to parents who would otherwise not be in a position to spare the children for attending classes.

❐

Bibliography

Addaval, S.B. (ed.): *India Year Book of Education Educational Research*, NCERT, New Delhi, 1998.

Aggarwal, J.C. : *National Policy on Education*, Arya Book Depot, New Delhi, 1979.

—*Development and Planning of Modern Education with Special Reference to India*, Vikas Publishing House, New Delhi, 1982.

Aparna Basu : *The Growth of Education and Development in India*, Oxford University Press, Delhi, 1970.

Buch, M.B. : *A Survey of Research in Education*, Centre of Advanced Study in Education, M.S. University of Baroda, Baroda, 1974.

Don Adams : *Education and Modernisation in Asia*, Addison Wesley Publishing Company, London, 1970.

Ehsanul Haq : *Education and Political Culture in India*, Sterling Publishers, New Delhi, 1981.

Ghosh, S.C. : *Educational Strategies in Developing Countries*, Sterling Publishers, New Delhi, 1976.

Goel, S.C. : *Education and Economic Growth in India*, The MacMillan Company of India Ltd., Delhi, 1975.

Gopinathan Nair, P.R.: *Primary Education, Population Growth and Socio-economic Change*, Allied Publishers, New Delhi, 1981.

Gore, M.S. : *History of Education in India,* NCERT, New Delhi, 1979.

Hatch, Ramend, N. and Steffle, Buford: *Administration of Education : History,* Englewood Cliffs, New Jersey, Prentice Hall, 1992.

Inarndar, N .R.: *Educational Administration,* Popular Prakashan, Mumbai, 1994.

Iqbal Narain, K.C. Pande and Mohan Lal Sarma: *Educational Administration,* Aalakli Publishers, Jaipur, 1976.

James, A.R. : *Vocation, Education and Guidance*: A System for the Seventies, Columbus, Charles E. Marril Publishing Co., Ohio, 1970.

John W., Hanson and Cole S. Brem Beck: *Education and the Development of Nations,* Holt, Rinehart and Winston, New York, 1966.

John Vaizey: *Education in Past, Penguin,* London, 1966.

Jones, A.J. : *Principles of Guidance and Pupil Personnel Work,* McGraw Hill, New York, 1963.

Joshi, R.N.: *Education-Elsewhere and Here,* Bharatiya Vidya Bhavan, Mumbai, 1979.

Julian, E., Butter Worth and Howard A. Dawson: *Modern History of Education,* McGraw Hill, New York, 1952.

Kamat, A.R. : *Educational History,* People's Publishing House, New Delhi, 1993.

Kidd, J.R. : *Education : Historical Perspective,* Indian Education Association, New Delhi, 1999.

Kochhar, S.K. : *Pivotal Issues in Indian Education,* Sterling, New Delhi, 1981.

Lakshmana Swamy Mudaliar A.: *Education in India,* Asia Publishing House, Mumbai, 1960.

Miller, Carroll H. : *Foundations of Education,* Harper and Brothers, New York, 1961.

Mukherji, SN.: *Administration of Education in India,* Acharya Book Depot, Baroda, 1962.

Naik, J.P. : *Education since Independence,* Vikas Publishing House, New Delhi, 1989.

Nairn, C.R. : *Policy and Performance in Indian Education,* Dr. K.G. Saiyidain Memorial Trust, New Delhi, 1999.

Naiq, J.P. : *Educational Planning in India,* Allied Publishers, Mumbai, 2001.

Noor, M.K. : *Elementary Education in India,* Allied Publishers, Mumbai, 2003.

—*The National Education Policy 1947-2000,* Ministry of Education and Social Welfare, Government of India. New Delhi, 2002.

Niblett, W.R. : *Essential Education,* University of London, London, 1955.

Nural Hasan, S. : *Challenges in Education, Culture and Social Welfare,* Allied Publishers, Mumbai, 1977.

Oldhan, J.N. : *Histonj of Education in India,* Oxford University Press, London, 1993.

Ohlsen, M.M. : *History of Education, Holt Rinehart and Winston,* New York, 2001.

Panchamukhi, P.R. : *Primary Education in India,* NCERT, 1990.

Paulo Freire : *Education : The Practice of Freedom,* Writers and Readers Publishing Co-operative, London, 1976.

Prem Kripal : *A Decade of Education in India,* Indian Book Company, Delhi, 1968.

Premi, M.K. : *Educational Planning in India,* Sterling Publishers, New Delhi, 1972.

Rajagopal, M.V. : *Kothari Commission,* Vidyardhi Prachuranalu, Machilipatnam, 1977.

Raju, V.B.: *Commentaries on the Constitution of India,* Eastern Book Company, Lucknow, 1973.

Rudolph & Rudolph : *Education and Politics in India,* Harvard University Press, Cambridge, 2002.

Russell, Bertrand: *Education and the Social Order,* Unwin, London, 1977.

Sharma, G.S.: *Education and Development,* ICSSR, New Delhi, 1973.

Shipman, M.D.: *Education and Modernisation,* Faber and Faber, London, 1971.

Shrimali, K.L.: *A Search for Values in Indian Education,* Vikas Publishers, Delhi, 1974

Shri Prakash: *Educational System of India : An Econometric Study,* Concept Publishing Company, Delhi, 1977.

Shukla, PD. : *Towards the New Pattern of Education in India,* Sterling Publishers, New Delhi, 1976.

Singh, Amarjit : *Is Intelligence Inherited?—A Critical Synthesis and Review of Research Findings,* NCERT, New Delhi, 1978.

Singla M.M. : *The Constitution of India-Studies in Perspective,* The World Press, Calcutta, 1975,

Siqueira, TN.: *The Education of India—History and Problems,* Oxford University Press, London, 1952.

Tiwari, D.D. : *Thoughts on Education,* Chugh Publications, Allahabad, 1972.

Venkatasubramanian, K. : *Education and Learning in India,* N. Vidyaranya Swamy, Secunderabad, 1999.

❐

Index

K

L

M

N

R

S

T

U

❑